Nature of the Rainforest

Costa Rica and Beyond

Nature of the Rainforest
Costa Rica and Beyond

Adrian Forsyth
Photographs by Michael Fogden and Patricia Fogden

Foreword by E. O. Wilson

A Zona Tropical Publication
from Comstock Publishing Associates
a division of Cornell University Press
Ithaca and London

Portions of this book appeared previously in Portraits of the Rainforest, 1990, by Camden House Publishing. The current edition first published 2008 by Zona Tropical Publications and by Cornell University Press.

Library of Congress Cataloging-in-Publication Data

Forsyth, Adrian.
  Nature of the rainforest : Costa Rica and beyond / Adrian Forsyth ; photographs by Michael Fogden and Patricia Fogden ; foreword by E.O. Wilson.
      p. cm.
  ISBN 978-0-8014-7475-0 (pbk. : alk. paper)
  1. Rain forest ecology--Costa Rica. 2. Rain forest animals--Costa Rica. 3. Rain forest plants--Costa Rica. I. Fogden, Michael. II. Fogden, Patricia. III. Title.

  QH108.C6F67 2008
  577.34097286--dc22

2008019291

Zona Tropical ISBN: 978-0-9798804-2-1

Printed in China

Book design: Zona Creativa, S.A.
Designer: Gabriela Wattson

Paperback printing   10 9 8 7 6 5 4 3

Photograph facing title page: cloud forest in Monteverde, Costa Rica
Photograph facing contents page: waterfall at Llanos de Cortes, Guanacaste, Costa Rica

This book is dedicated to the memory of Barbara D'Achille, journalist, environmentalist, and friend. In her effort to communicate the natural beauty of Peru to its people, D'Achille made the ultimate sacrifice for conservation.

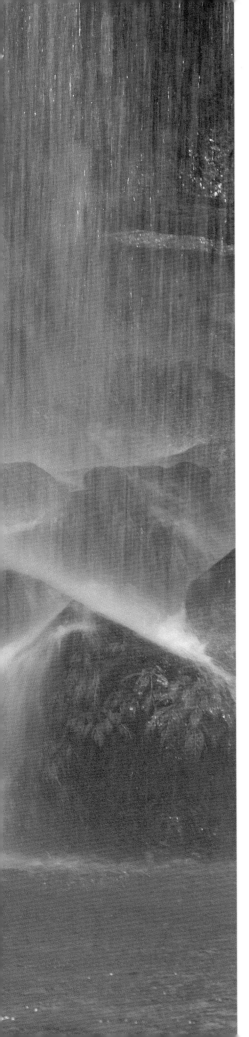

Contents

Forest of dreams
A foreword by E. O. Wilson

Conservationist Aldo Leopold's observation that the ecologist lives in a world of wounds bears a special poignancy with regard to the tropics. Already, virgin wilderness is almost unattainable. To watch a naked Amerindian stand in an unpolluted stream and hunt fish with bow and arrow in the Pleistocene manner, as Adrian Forsyth has done, requires both determination and luck.

The Stone Age peoples of the world who have managed to survive influenza and venereal disease are down to a few tens of thousands and are being quickly furnished with guns and Disneyland T-shirts even as they are driven from their land. The forests around them are felled and burned with greedy abandon. The tropical rainforest today covers only 6 percent of the land surface of the world, down nearly half from its original extent. It is being removed at the rate of about 1 percent a year, or 39,000 square miles (100,000 km²)—equal to the size of a football field per second. Put another way, the rainforest covers an area roughly that of the United States, and human activity is destroying an area equal to that of South Carolina each year. The book you have in your hands is thus in imminent danger of becoming more a historical document than a Baedeker of the tropical environment.

Why should anyone care? That is the point of this collection of essays. An academic ecologist with long experience in the tropics, Forsyth contributes with this book to the genuine literature of ecology, wherein exact knowledge is expressed through the prisms of disciplined emotion. Such writing requires a rare combination of scientific training and metaphorical skill, and Forsyth displays the instincts of a creative writer, taking us deep into the tropical rainforest.

Most of the world's biological diversity, as Forsyth points out, lives in rainforests. Biologists have described and put scientific names on 1.4 million species in all parts of the world, but they emphasize that this is only a small fraction of the actual number, which probably lies somewhere between 10 million and 80 million. With more than half of the species residing in rainforests, it can be conservatively estimated that more than one-quarter of all the species in the world will vanish during the next fifty years. To see what that means close up, consider the amazing density of life and the restricted distribution of plant and animal forms described by Forsyth in the mountain cloud forests of the eastern Andean slopes. When a mountain ridge in Ecuador was cleared—a routine operation nowadays in South America—thirty-eight plant species limited to the ridge at once became extinct.

Palaeontologists have recorded five episodes of mass extinction during the past 600 million years, the length of time spanning the history of modern life-forms in the sea and on land. The present spasm, which includes the destruction of rainforests and other rich natural habitats, is the sixth episode and potentially the most dangerous for life as a whole: Not only does the cut promise to be deeper, but for the first time, even plant species are being eliminated in large numbers. A further warning: The average life span of a species and its descendants in the past has been from 1 to 10 million years, depending on group. The time required for the loss in diversity to be restored by natural species formation following previous episodes has been 5 to 10 million years.

All this tells us that humanity is carelessly throwing away the Creation and relinquishing the chance to regain it. In order to appreciate the magnitude of that loss and to stanch it so that future generations may not curse our name, we must learn more about life on Earth, and we must learn it quickly. The tropical rainforest is vastly more than jungles and bugs. It is a treasure house of resources and a cathedral of organic complexity. It will be a potential source of wonder and an aesthetic thrill for all time to come if we refrain from burning it down and letting it wash to the sea.

For these reasons, this book represents much more than simple nature writing. It calls attention to the best of this planet and to the compelling reasons why we should look south, inland, to the forest of dreams. Then we can remember in the deepest sense where this race came from and why life itself, and not just Earth, is home.

E. O. Wilson

The protected forests of the Monteverde Cloud Forest Preserve support many of Costa Rica's 850 species of birds, 700 species of butterflies, and 200 species of mammals. But outside of protected parks and reserves tropical forests are being destroyed at an alarming rate.

Preface
Flower for a day

A spring morning here is announced by the loud, excessively cheerful chorusing of the clay-colored robins that forage in the patch of pasture below the cabin. Today, their rudely saccharine effect is tempered by the hoarse, rumbling protestations of howler monkeys in the forest that surrounds us. I feel the way the howlers sound this cool morning. My damp field clothes are clammy as I pull them on over stiff limbs. The sun still hides behind the eastern hills, and hot coffee is sorely needed. Photographer Michael Fogden, the owner of the accommodation, attends to this dependency first. Soon, we are outside on the birding bench that overlooks the mountainous landscape, hands cupped around warm mugs, letting the infusion of sugar, caffeine, and complex alkaloids do its vitalizing work. There is no need to move just yet. From this perch, Michael has identified some 220 species of birds, and two hours of excellent, completely sedentary birding lie ahead.

From the porch, I can see that it is a rare day, a *Sobralia* day. Below us, the landscape is one vast composition imbued with every shade of green. But this morning, the tree crowns are emblazoned here and there with clumps of huge, white orchid blossoms that catch the morning sun. They are *Sobralia*, massive orchids that bloom en masse for one brief and unpredictable day. By tomorrow morning, the fragile petals will have faded; they seem to self-digest once their single day is done.

Entire populations of *Sobralia* orchids growing in the rainforest canopy open their large snow-white blossoms in unison. But the fragile blossoms survive for only a single day.

Overhead, a flock of parrots races, calling out the sound of the tropics. Without looking, Michael identifies them as brown-hooded parrots—birds distinguished by voices more musical and less raucous than those of other parrots—and I try to absorb both the sound and yet another bit of Michael's ornithological expertise. We watch a succession of small birds taking rewards that plants normally confer upon ants. A scarlet-thighed dacnis drinks at the extrafloral nectaries of an *Inga* treelet sprouting up in front of the porch. The *Cecropia* tree, which produces tiny white Müllerian bodies in brown velvet glandular patches under its leaf stems for the *Azteca* ants that defend its leaves, is being robbed by seedeaters, bananaquits, and parulas that pluck the bodies with rapid-fire pecks. They are joined by a chestnut-sided warbler that must be fattening up for its impending journey north, back to the scrubby old fields and second-growth forests of southern Canada and New England.

Below us is a stand of *Pothomorphe* piper plants—succulent, erect treelets with dinner-plate-sized leaves that smell of licorice. Hidden in their tangle, a nightingale wren begins its song. Its whistle starts high and then drops lower, then up, now a shade away, following a slow, even cadence, setting up a pattern that seems to be random and new each time but that always follows the same jagged, jazzlike avoidance of melody.

At 8 a.m., the bird chorus begins to wane as the cicadas wax louder and shriller, proclaiming the time to pull on boots and move. Michael and I want to see different things, so we go our own ways. Two is always a crowd if you hope to see any wildlife or to take your time with your own particular fascinations. I look for treehoppers and other insects. Michael probably has a special bird or snake in mind.

The day yields little new in the way of treehoppers. But it hardly matters. I take pleasure in the spectacle created by the *Diospyros* persimmon trees, which now bear heavy crops of orange fruit. The abundance is too much for the ungainly crested guans, birds the size of turkeys that thrash about, dislodging fruit as they forage. Below one tree, a mass of fallen fruit ferments; I find six large, iridescent blue butterfly wings and guess that a passing jacamar has taken unfair advantage of the fruit-drunk morphos.

By noon, the river beckons. The rushing water pauses and eddies here and there in clear, deep pools tinted pale blue. It is cool enough to dispel any sense of midday torpor. Along the banks is an unfamiliar plant, a member of the same family as coffee, with a creamy white, 4-inch-long (10 cm), trumpet-shaped flower that ends in a mandala of wavy petals and exudes a scent of jasmine. Huge black carpenter bees buzz in red melastoma flowers the size of roses. A white hawk, a ghostly bird that haunts the dark edge of the forest, perches unobtrusively on a limb, patiently watching for a snake to risk a sunbath.

At around four o'clock in the afternoon, the band-backed wrens begin again to chatter and scold. A flock of chestnut-headed oropendolas, highly social relatives of orioles, stages a concert in black and yellow, wheeling and circling through the clearing below the cabin, calling noisily. Soon, they settle on a tree crown and embark on an extended, more intimate dialogue with distinctive liquid songs that sound like gurgling, dripping water. These are the sounds of social interaction, the greetings of one's own kind, and they mark the time for me to return, to sit once more on the bench admiring the sweep of the landscape after the confines of the forest. As always, we commemorate the day with an aromatic drink or two of rum.

Below us, the humid breath of untold billions of leaves begins to cool and condense. From the forest, a spotted woodcreeper calls. Its sinking, mournful notes express the mood—the unspeakable sadness of mist and cloud gathering soft and gray on the thickly forested hills, of dusk settling down the valley as it has done for countless days and years. Away on the farthest northeastern ridge, we can see a swath of pasture, the frayed edge of this island of forest.

Almost every reflective moment of a day like this in Peñas Blancas is attended by a mixture of hope and trepidation. A few years ago, chain saws were busy felling the trees, converting the valley into sodden, unproductive pasture. Now, as the result of a joint conservation effort by Costa Ricans and people from the United States, Canada, and Europe, much of the forest is protected. The wildlife is bouncing back after decades of hunting: the collared peccary population is growing; hard on its heels is the burgeoning cat population. More support is pouring in to maintain this watershed. The entire country is counting on these forests to capture and regulate the flow of water into its Lake Arenal hydroelectric system, a billion-dollar installation that generates half of Costa Rica's electricity and much of its irrigation water. But just beyond the reserve, deforestation proceeds, driven by the combined forces of human population growth and poorly planned—or unplanned—economic development.

The long, tweezerlike bill of the rufous-tailed jacamar, above, is well suited to catching long-winged insects, such as dragonflies and butterflies. Even fast-flying morphos (*Morpho peleides*), right, are often taken by jacamars.

I know the family of the man cutting that distant ridge. A generation ago, the patriarch, a landless *campesino*, rode into these mountains on a makeshift trail. With his wife, he produced twenty children, all of them still living, all of them married, all with children of their own. Their family reunion could fill a village. In this family, too, I have seen the mix of optimism and apprehension that surrounds tropical conservation. The brother of the man clearing the pasture on the ridge once worked for me cutting trails. Before that, he felled more than his share of the Arenal Forest Reserve. He moved on to capitalize on the ecotourism trade that the nearby Monteverde Cloud Forest Preserve has created and now makes a much better living by renting horses and guiding tourists. He has two children, and that is plenty, he says. These are hopeful signs. But I can remember a trip we made not long ago to the other side of this valley. As we stood overlooking the watershed above Lake Arenal, I commented that there was still a lot of forest on these slopes. "Too much," he replied.

Although he makes his living from the tourist traffic to the forest reserve and gets his electricity from its runoff, my friend grew up believing that pasture is progress, that untouched forest is a sign of underdevelopment and rural poverty. His is not an isolated, backwater mentality but the same prevailing belief that guides the urbane and powerful politicians, economists, bankers, and religious leaders and informs the agricultural, industrial, and urban cultures they direct. The leaders of modern society are well educated in the liberal arts, in economics, in technology. But what value do they place on the woodcreeper's lament or on the *Sobralia*, which bloom for a single day and can never be bought or sold?

Long ago, conservationist Aldo Leopold observed that the land-use practices that resulted in habitat destruction were the consequence of economics. He also argued that "economic laws may be permanent, but their impact reflects what people want, which in turn reflects what they know and what they are." This book seeks, in a small way, to change what people know and what they want. Communicating something of the intricate beauty of the rainforest will not be enough to guarantee its survival. But it is part of the incremental process of altering the human understanding and appreciation of nature. All the other components—institution-building, debt reduction, aid for sustainable development, improved planning, scientific research—necessary to make the preservation of tropical forest technically and materially possible will not be enough if an interest in nature does not exist in the hearts and minds of people.

Any sketch of a subject so profoundly diverse, created with a few thousand words and a few hundred photographs, must give a biased view. In this book, we confine most of our mate-

rial to the New World tropics, with special emphasis on Costa Rica and Peru. We confess without apology to being anecdotal and speculative; these activities are a large part of the enjoyment of tropical natural history. But we also attempt to cover some classic themes that have long fascinated tropical biologists: the importance of diversity, mimicry, the wealth of species, and nutrient cycles. Some of the chapters are oriented toward specific organisms: the sloths so specialized for life in the treetops; the snakes that haunt the thoughts of rainforest residents and visitors alike. Other chapters try to trace ecological connections and patterns. Comparisons with the temperate zone are made for a reason: The fate of these unique tropical habitats depends on the will and resources of people from both North and South.

We have tried to proselytize by bringing words and images together in a portrait of the rainforest. If we could, we would bring the sounds, the tastes, the textures, and the smells as well. But perhaps it is better that you acquire these for yourself.

The clouds and mists that create tropical rainforests and sustain their diverse life-forms are themselves created by the forests, left. The evaporative transpiration of the trees and other plants is important in forming clouds and in maintaining the climatic patterns of forested regions.

The gorgeous blooms of the scarlet passionflower (*Passiflora vitifolia*), right, are visited and pollinated by hermit hummingbirds.

Roots of diversity
The origins of tropical variety

As the Manú River percolates through the eastern foothills of the Peruvian Andes, it comes to resemble a giant stream of *café con leche*. Carrying a surprising burden of suspended silt and sand as it wends its way toward the Amazon, the Manú both erodes and builds the floodplain. The current carves away the bank on the river's outward curves and lays down beaches on its inward curves. These beaches come and go, disappearing under the muddy flood during the rains and emerging once more during dry season.

In August, when the new crop of sugar-sand beaches stands high and sunbaked, a handsome and instructive set of birds begins to nest. Sand-colored nighthawks insert their cryptically mottled selves among the boldly patterned black skimmers and cool white terns. Orinoco geese bare their russet-orange chests. There is an ecological familiarity to this association of birds that any temperate-zone naturalist will recognize, and it offers an interesting contrast to the adjacent forest.

Each bird in this decidedly tropical place seems to be an ecological replica of a temperate-zone counterpart. Swallows much like northern tree swallows nest in the emergent skeletons of drowned trees, foraging back and forth above the river and gleaning, as swallows do everywhere, the invisible drift of tiny insects. A cocoi heron, with the size and regal demeanor of the northern great blue heron but tailored in elegant gray with black and white calligraphy on its chest, stalks the shallows, always alone. More sociable sandpipers take smaller fry. And just as they do along the eastern seaboard, the black skimmers doze in full sun. They leave it to the kingfishers to dive for the fish that stay low by day. The skimmers begin to glide in the soft light of dusk and carry on by the light of the moon and stars, using their elongated, protruding lower bills to chisel up small fish dawdling at the surface. Geese browse the succulent sprouts greening the new edge of the landscape.

The birds on the beaches of Manú employ the same feeding behaviors as birds on the sandy shores of the more extreme latitudes of the northern hemisphere. The terns here are just as pugnaciously defensive as they are everywhere, rising up noisily at your approach and swooping just above your head so that you feel the breath of their angry wings. A yellow-billed tern hovers above the water, a beating band of light like a letter M dancing against the green backdrop of trees; then it twists head down and lifts its wings to set off the vertical plunge. It emerges with a silver minnow held sideways in its pastel yellow bill.

In all these aspects, the community of birds along the beaches of the Manú seems comparable to the bird community one might find sharing a beach on, for example, Cape Cod. To be sure, there are a few exclusively tropical niceties on Manú's beaches, such as the bizarre horned screamers with their ornamented heads. Yet even they waddle in pairs and feed much like geese. For the most part, this tropical habitat supports a bird community close to that of its temperate counterpart.

The rainforests of upper Amazonia, adjoining the foothills of the Andes, are home to the greatest diversity of plants and animals on earth. Amazonia's rainforest is the most diverse of all tropical forests and a few square miles may harbor as many as 500 species of birds, 80 varieties of frogs, and several hundred species of trees. Vast areas of unbroken Amazonian forest still remain.

Once you step into the forest, however, the apparent similarities vanish. The number of bird species and the richness of their behaviors take on uniquely tropical dimensions. There are more breeding birds in the Amazonian rainforest than in any other place on Earth. If we total up the numbers of breeding bird species in different parts of the globe, we see that Amazonia is the end point of a trend in which species richness accelerates as we approach the equator from north or south. If we compare areas of roughly the same size, Greenland rings in with 56 breeding species, Labrador 81, Newfoundland 118, New York State 195, Guatemala 469, Panama 1,100, and Colombia 1,395.

In this regard, birds are not exceptional. Most terrestrial life-forms increase in species diversity as one moves from higher latitudes toward the equator. I can collect hundreds of butterflies in the fields and forests around my Ontario residence in a day, but my collection might embrace only a few dozen species. Manú probably holds a thousand species. A count done in an Amazonian rainforest found 283 tree species in 2.5 acres (1 hectare).

For comparison, there are few natural forests in temperate zones where one could find more than a couple of dozen tree species on the same amount of land. Animal-diversity differences are even greater. For example, on one individual tree from the area just south of Manú, a collection of ants identified by biologist E. O. Wilson yielded forty-three species, more than occur in all of the British Isles. Perhaps the most fundamental challenge of tropical ecology is to account for this bewildering diversity, the ecological and genetic variety that is the hallmark and glory of tropical rainforests.

Leading into the forest from one of the beaches along the Manú is a transect trail where ecologists and ornithologists such as John Terborgh, John Fitzpatrick, Charles Munn, Scott Robinson, and assorted colleagues have recorded more than five hundred bird species. The trail slices through the successional sequence that is left as the riverbed winds across the alluvial plain. One abruptly passes from pure sun beating on a low monoculture of sunflowers that springs up on the virgin sand into the sudden shade created by a wall of giant *Gynerium* cane, which itself fades into stands of lush heliconia and ginger.

Figs and other weedy pioneer trees dominate the next successional phase, and then the trail moves into the upland forest above the floodplain. Where the most diverse temperate forest might support forty bird species, the same area of forest along the Manú supports six times as many.

Ecological diversity proliferates in the forest. In addition to more widespread sorts of birds such as flycatchers, vireos, tanagers, woodpeckers, warblers, pigeons, and the like, the birder will meet leaftossers, toucans, motmots, tinamous, manakins, macaws, nunbirds, antbirds, becards, trumpeters, giant ground-cuckoos—birds that have no ecological counterparts in northern forests.

Before any ecological explanation of the state of the world is given, caveats are in order: history and geography play a role in influencing diversity. By a quirk of evolutionary fate, bromeliads—for example, the pineapple family of some two thousand species—flourish only in neotropical rainforests, having never evolved or established themselves in Africa and Asia. The forests there are no doubt the poorer for it. Floras and faunas from North America and South America are still mingling as a result of the emergence of the Panamanian land bridge millions of years ago. Something of a region's variety will be owing to the history of such an exchange. Speciation rates are influenced by geography—areas such as the Andean foothills are extraordinarily rich in endemic species, and their generation may cause Ecuadoran rainforests to have greater diversity than more distant Brazilian forests. Of the larger, slower evolutionary processes, we have but an inkling. It is easier to look at ecological correlations of diversity.

John Terborgh has tried to answer the question, What ecological factors allow so many bird species to share an Amazonian rainforest? The beaches where his Manú transect begins provide a revealing starting point for a temperate-tropical comparison.

The absence of any profound difference in the temperate and tropical bird communities found on a beach is a result of a fundamental physical and ecological similarity in the habitats. This habitat provides only a simple two-dimensional nesting surface and a volume of water in which to feed. In both places, the birds have essentially the same limited spectrum of resources to divide up. By contrast, temperate and tropical forests, although superficially alike in being composed of large trees, offer a radically different spectrum of resources.

Ornithologists pay much attention to food resources and with good reason. Being small, warm-blooded organisms, birds spend a great deal of their day hunting for food; indeed, studies show that competition for food and for territories that contain food is a dominant feature of avian life. It is not surprising, then, that food diversity is a key to tropical bird diversity. Tropical rainforests offer food resources not found in temperate forests. For example, a large number of tropical-forest birds are specialized followers of army ants; a great radiation of antbirds, ovenbirds, and woodcreepers gleans the insects stirred up by army-ant raids. Although some army ants make it into the temperate zones, they are exclusively subterranean and so offer no such opportunity for temperate-forest birds.

Tropical bird communities are much more diverse than temperate communities and include species with diets that are unrepresented in northern forests. The collared araçari, left, and other toucans feed on a diverse selection of fruits throughout the year, while the broad-billed motmot, above, and relatives specialize in large-bodied insects, such as katydids, cicadas, and beetles.

Many tropical birds are frugivores that take advantage of the year-round occurrence of fruit in tropical forests. Such a resource is available only at certain times in temperate forests—and in dry tropical habitats, for that matter—and thus only in tropical rainforests is there a great proliferation of frugivores such as cotingids. Terborgh compared Manú's avifauna with that of a prime hardwood forest in South Carolina, one of the richest forests left in the temperate zone. Of the forty species breeding in that temperate forest, only seven species included significant amounts of fruit and nectar in their diet. In Manú, eighty-four species make use of fruit and nectar.

Dead leaves are another resource that has a uniquely tropical importance. They are always present in rainforests and act as hideouts for many insects. Accordingly, there is a guild of birds in tropical forests that always searches in dead leaves. No temperate birds use this technique as their primary food-foraging behavior.

In fact, none of the foregoing life-history options are available in the temperate zone. But when Terborgh toted up the contribution of these tropical foraging strategies, he found that they account for only about one-third of the increased forest-bird diversity in the tropics.

Another 17 percent of Manú's avian diversity is due to birds that specialize in feeding on large insects. In both temperate-zone forests and the tropics, the majority of birds are insectivores, at least when they are breeding. But in contrast to temperate insectivores, many tropical birds such as motmots and nunbirds are specialized predators of small vertebrate animals and huge insects like katydids. I once watched a motmot swoop down to grab a *Dichotomius* dung scarab, a beetle so strong that it is virtually impossible to hold in one's fist because it burrows and claws its way through one's fingers. The beetle is nearly the size of a walnut, and its layers of corrugated black chitin make it almost as heavily armored. The motmot picked up the beetle with its heavy, forcepslike, slightly serrated bill, flew up to its stout perch and vigorously smacked the beetle up and down and back and forth on the limb until it was thoroughly tenderized. I could hear the beetle cracking under the bludgeoning force. Temperate insectivores simply do not do that sort of thing. A turkey's crushing gizzard might be up to tackling such an item, but few other temperate-forest birds could handle it. And unlike turkeys, motmots are able to swoop down on terrestrial crabs and to snag lizards, especially anole lizards, from tree trunks. In short, tropical birds such as motmots, anis,

Above, a hairy-legged nectar bat visits a flowering bromeliad (*Werauhia nephrolepis*) to feed on nectar. Most temperate-zone bats are insectivorous, but many tropical species exploit other foods, including nectar, fruit, fish, and blood.

Most temperate-zone orchids grow on the ground, but in the tropics, tens of thousands of orchid species, including these *Oncidium macranthum* from Ecuador, left, grow as epiphytes. High levels of humidity and rainfall as well as freedom from frost allow epiphytes to flourish in the rainforest.

and nunbirds consume prey items in a size range that is largely absent from the temperate woods.

Half the diversity of Manú's forest avifauna appears to exist simply by virtue of greater ecological specialization. The subdivision of physical space is an obvious factor in packing species together in ecological communities. Bird species are often ecologically separated by search-and-capture behaviors that, in turn, are related to the structure of the vegetation where they occur. Robert MacArthur, a founder of the study of community ecology, showed that structure in the forest environment is an important contributor to diversity. Some birds forage in the tree crowns, some in the midstrata, and others in the understory or on the ground. Certainly, a tall rainforest offers more height than does a temperate hardwood forest. But no one who studies tropical birds, including Terborgh, believes that the height of the trees accounts for most of the ecological segregation in the rainforest.

To my mind, far more important than mere height is the fact that tropical rainforest trees can support epiphytes—plants that grow on other plants, which are freed from having to connect with the earth, and which grow in shapes and locations unused by temperate plants. Lianas rise from the forest floor, free-swinging like twisted ship's cables, until they grasp a limb and begin to run laterally through the canopy. Stringier vines plaster their leaves against the trunk. Inspection of their leaves reveals algae, lichens, and mosses. Clusters of ferns, dangling cacti, carpets of heathlike shrubs, and small trees wholly lacking contact with the soil can be seen on the bole and limbs of the tree.

After spending any time in the tropics, you tend to take the vegetation for granted. But when you return to the temperate forest, you are struck by its stark, nakedly austere characteristics. Coastal forests of the temperate zone may be hung and speckled with epiphytic mosses and lichens, but it is only in the tropics that the higher plants begin colonizing, climbing, and carpeting every solid surface, from tree buttresses and boles to limbs and leaves. It is the higher plant epiphytes that give tropical vegetation its exuberant appearance and that are a basic component of tropical diversity.

Epiphytes number some 30,000 species in 850 genera and 65 plant families. In tropical rainforests and cloud forests, epiphytes account for 34 to 63 percent of the total number of plant species. In cloud forests, epiphytes reach their full potential, making up 40 percent of the total plant biomass. Important plant families such as the orchids are primarily epiphytic, and they achieve this state only in the tropics. All temperate-zone orchids are dependent on soil for a water supply to replenish the moisture lost during evapotranspiration. Yet in tropical rainforests, although orchids do grow on the ground, vastly more grow as epiphytes—20,000 species, according to one count. In their elevated niches, orchids assume a fantastic diversity of growth forms, from sprawling vines and dangling, ropelike strands to bushy clumps with massive leaves and compact, mossy growths that carpet the uppermost twisted, wind-raked tree limbs. A survey of a single tree in a Venezuelan rainforest revealed a community of 47 different species of epiphytic orchids.

What makes epiphytism possible on such a grand scale is the same thing that is responsible for the diversity of rainforests: a damp and invariably warm atmosphere. The argument is an old

A male violet-tailed sylph feeds at an epiphytic blueberry (*Psammisia* sp.). In rainforests and cloud forests, many species of blueberry are found growing high above the ground in the canopy, where they provide a year-round supply of nectar for hummingbirds.

one and is probably too prosaically mechanical for most ecologists to find attractive. They have variously debated whether greater productivity, predation rates, evolutionary time, speciation rates, climatic stability, and other forces have generated high tropical diversity. All of these may be factors, but the tropical diversity the naturalist encounters on the ground stems from a climate that makes it possible.

Tropical plant growth-forms like strangler figs are possible only where there is freedom from the physical damage of freezing. An infant strangler fig growing high above the forest floor in the crotch of a tree may dangle its pencil-thick roots 165 feet (50 m) to the forest floor with no risk of ice exploding its delicate plumbing. Humidity makes things easier for leaves. In the midlevels of tropical rainforests, philodendron leaves the size of umbrellas grow on tree trunks, completely cut off from the soil. Northern aroids like jack-in-the-pulpit or skunk cabbage retain something of the

lushly huge leaves of their tropical relatives, but they are confined to moist, almost marshy shade because of the rate at which their leaves transpire water. Compare rainforest cacti with desert cacti. In the driest deserts, cacti grow as spiny columns or barrels that trade off a reduced photosynthetic surface area for a well-defended, highly reflective barrier against water loss and overheating. Desert cacti must have root contact with soil in order to draw up a store of water during the periods of moisture. In the rainforest, cacti are typically spine-free, and the stems can grow flattened out, leaflike, to intercept as much light as possible. They may send roots out from any stem section or have almost no roots at all simply because ambient moisture levels are so high.

It may be true that many tropical trees, especially those in the canopy, have the same unlobed oval leaf shape with a pronounced drip tip for shedding water. Yet the larger truth is that when all plants are considered, there is a fantastically greater array of leaf shapes and sizes in a tropical forest than in a temperate-zone forest. A rainforest's climatic constancy allows specialization and hence variety in design at all levels, from enzymes to gross architecture. Although rainfall is often seasonal in the tropics, other physical parameters are far more constant. At the equator, the maximum amount of sunlight in any day falls on the equinoxes, but that amount is only 13 percent greater than the minimum amount during the solstices. At temperate latitudes, say, 50 degrees, the difference between the minimum and maximum sunlight leaps to 400 percent. In the north, then, a plant must endure constantly changing day lengths, great temperature differences, and a profound waxing and waning of its energy supply. The temperature difference between night and day in a tropical rainforest is as great as the variation in the entire year. In a temperate zone, the temperature will fluctuate from as hot or hotter than any tropical rainforest to well below freezing. Such climatic variations encourage conformity in design. In extremely windy areas, all trees reach the same reduced height. In areas where rainfall fluctuates greatly, diversity falls off sharply and plants exist in a limited set of shapes and sizes.

If this climatic argument is true, there should be not only a temperate-tropical diversity gradient but also a relationship between rainfall, seasonality, and plant diversity in tropical forests. Botanist Al Gentry has surveyed plant-species counts for a number of tropical sites and found a strong correlation between rainfall and plant diversity. Wet forests were three times as diverse as dry forests, and moist forests were intermediate. Epiphyte diversity responded most strongly to rainfall, while lianas and large trees were little affected by changes in precipitation. The rate of increase is correspondingly greater for epiphytes, which is just what we would expect for plants that have no opportunity to draw on the great buffering reservoir of soil moisture.

Nor is it only plants that are offered more opportunities by a warm, rainy climate. Frogs are also freer in the rainforest, and a wide range of climbing tree frogs uses water-filled tree holes and epiphytes for breeding and feeding. This, in turn, makes life possible for crane hawks, which have double-jointed knees that bend both forward and backward, allowing them to stick their legs into tree holes in search of prey.

Because there are insects that feed on the leaves of epiphytes and the collections of humus and detritus that gather around their roots, tropical birds have a wide range of places to forage. Many tropical birds subdivide the unique structures offered by epiphyte communities such as lianas, another fundamentally tropical-forest feature. Two and a half acres (1 hectare) may contain more than 1,000 liana stems, which reach into the canopy and stretch from one tree crown to another; the forest is literally woven together by their resilient climbing, clinging tendrils and stems. This growth form composes about 20 percent of the forest's biomass and has become a site of specialization. Vine searchers—the various foliage gleaners and other ovenbird species—spend much of the time rummaging in their tangles.

Likewise, large radiations of climbing lizards such as anoles and geckos have followed their insect prey into the trees. Herpetologist Alan Pounds has studied montane rainforest anole communities in

Climbing lianas, left, are a prominent and important feature of tropical forests, providing arboreal pathways for a multitude of climbing animals.

Tropical rainforests are characterized by the great ecological specialization of many organisms, such as these male orchid bees (*Eulaema* sp.), above, visiting and pollinating an orchid (*Acineta chrysantha*). The bees collect perfumes that are later modified to provide sexual pheromones.

The crowned frog (*Anotheca spinosa*), found in Costa Rica, breeds in water-filled tank bromeliads that grow on the branches of montane rainforest trees. Such ecological specializations increase the vulnerability of this species to deforestation.

Costa Rica and found that they, too, have subdivided the forest structurally. Some species are canopy-specialized, while others segregate at various levels of the understory and at light gaps, such as those created by tree falls. Their body forms and movement patterns vary accordingly: there are runners, jumpers, and crawlers, depending on the sort of vegetation and substrate on which they live.

That particular diversity argument should not hold for groups such as terrestrial mammals that would be little affected by structures beyond their reach. Indeed, ground-dwelling mammals show little of the sharp diversity increase that epiphytes, birds, insects, and other organisms do as we approach the equator and move from dry to wet areas. Reinforcing this pattern is the fact that mammals such as bats, which can divide up the air space and tiers of the forest and which feed on the broader range of foods offered by the upper echelons of the forest, show the same sharp increase in species diversity as one moves from the temperate zone toward the equator. A study of the rainforest in Queensland, Australia, concluded that it is the structure of the vegetation itself that determines the organization of the community of bats found in the forest. Bats react to the pockets of space in the forest mosaic. Species with broad, maneuverable wings occupy the dense canopy; others with faster flight and long, narrow wings work the open spaces.

Such diversity patterns also hold for monkeys and other arboreal mammals that forage in the upper levels of the forest. Structural features like vine tangles offer domiciles for monkeys such as the pygmy marmoset, which lives in family groups, sucks tree sap, and retreats to the protective mazes when threatened. And the monkeys themselves support formidable birds such as harpy eagles and ornate hawk-eagles that are sit-and-wait predators of primates and other canopy mammals. They have no temperate-forest equivalent. This concatenation of diversity began with the climate and the plants that make arboreality possible.

It is not only the complex structure of the rainforest flora that is important. The larger significance of greater plant diversity is that each species opens additional means of subdividing the environment for shelter as well as for foraging sites. Over the years, the epiphytes build up a mat of humus on tree limbs that acts as a foraging ground for canopy specialists like ochraceous wrens, which root there for beetle and fly larvae. But the epiphytes also provide resources for a range of herbivorous insects such as leaf-mining flies and flower-eating caterpillars. The flowers supply nectar, oil, and perfume for bees, flies, hummingbirds, and butterflies. The fruits are eaten by birds and mammals.

Consider the tank bromeliads, which add both structural complexity and aquatic microhabitats to the upper echelons of the forest. Costa Rican biologist Claudio Picado surveyed the fauna found in tank bromeliads and toted up an amazing two hundred and fifty species. In addition to a rich resident fauna of mosquitoes, midges, and syrphid flies, tank bromeliads provide breeding sites for the spectacular giant damselfly. The damselfly feeds on the other insects and possibly on the tadpoles that live in the tanks. The adult has a 7.5-inch (17 cm) wingspan, which exceeds that of all other damselflies and enables the insect to specialize in hovering delicately in front of an orb-weaving spiderweb for an indelicate meal: it plucks out the spider and consumes its abdomen. But the most

The gliding leaf frog (*Agalychnis spurrelli*), above left, can glide at angles of 45°, enabling it to move easily from tree to tree in the forest canopy and to escape arboreal predators.

The spectacular giant, or helicopter, damselfly (*Megaloprepus coerulatus*), above right, is a specialist predator of spiders. It uses tank bromeliads as sites to lay its eggs.

remarkable feature of this damselfly is the almost hallucinatory effect it creates when it is encountered in the forest. Its wings are transparent save for a bold dab of blue or yellow pigment on each wing tip, and its thin, dark body is virtually invisible. Its forewings and hind wings beat out of phase so that only the dancing spots of color are seen bouncing back and forth as it moves slowly and mysteriously through the shady understory.

In spite of the damselfly nymphs, *Dendrobates* frogs place their tadpoles (and other frogs lay their eggs) in bromeliads, a development that has led to tree frogs such as *Hyla zeteki* relying on the eggs of others as their primary food. Stretched-out lizards are found in bromeliads, and their body forms appear suited for reaching far down into the recessed crevices in search of insect larvae. Hummingbirds pollinate the bold inflorescences. Skipper butterfly caterpillars feed on bromeliad leaves, and in the Andes, spectacled bears pull down the leaves to eat the soft, blanched bases.

Bromeliads may be an exceptionally small ecosystem, but the net result of adding any plant to an ecosystem is the triggering of an ecological multiplier effect. In thus praising plants, we should not forget that adding an animal to an ecosystem allows

for the same result. Every vertebrate in a tropical forest is host to an abundance of parasites. That is something you can observe firsthand, whether you want to or not. Most people initially experience the richness of tropical parasites in the form of a microbial assault on the digestive tract. But every once in a while, something more distinctly tropical establishes a foothold.

A couple of years ago, I went hiking in Costa Rica wearing rubber boots that were oversized and leaky besides. It was raining, and the trail was a mixture of muck and rock. Eventually, the ends of my smaller toes became blistered from the slogging. After a few days had passed, the blisters toughened, a protective callus formed and I forgot all about them. Some weeks later, I was back in Ontario and noticed that all my toes had reverted to their normal state save the smallest one on my right foot. This little pinkie was still callused on the end and had a dull, hollow feel to it. I left it alone for a time, but when the condition persisted, I thought it wise to investigate. For my studies, I had in hand a sharp, clean pair of forceps but no particular expectations. I jabbed experimentally at the callused mass, and it erupted. A mass of creamy, pinkish yellow eggs, like fish roe, burst out of the skin and hung there inelegantly on the end of my toe. After a few shocked seconds of puzzlement and contemplation, a light went on in my head. "A toe flea," I exclaimed with a mixture of horror and satisfaction.

For years, I had read about the so-called niguas, chigoes, and jiggers (not to be confused with chiggers). Jiggers gained notoriety by attacking the feet of the first explorers of Latin America, who duly recorded their travails for their many readers. I had finally experienced that famous flea. *Tunga penetrans* is specialized and can be picked up when one goes barefoot, especially in the light, sandy soils frequented by farm livestock such as pigs. Females of this flea burrow into mammals, especially pigs, rats, and humans. Safely ensconced below the hide, they tap into the bloodstream and begin growing an egg mass. They swell prodigiously, reaching the size of a pea before bursting the well-formed larval fleas out into the environment, where they pupate.

The toe flea exemplifies the multiplier effect associated with parasitism. Like all parasites, it is an extreme anatomical specialist and lives within or subsists on a single individual, so each host species can be used by many different parasites. A predator, by contrast, typically lives on many individuals drawn from several prey species and thus has to be a generalist. Parasites, then, are more diverse than their larger host organisms. Vertebrate predators in a tropical rainforest are not excessively richer than those in drier or more temperate habitats, but parasites are exceedingly rich. Ecologist Peter Price has estimated that half of all species on Earth are parasitic. Neotropical vertebrates, especially mammals and birds, all carry with them vast collections of specialized mites, ticks, lice, and sucking wingless flies. Even the sleek-skinned snakes harbor an extensive collection of specialized ticks. Many primary parasites transmit secondary parasites that cause ailments like leishmaniasis, malaria, and Chagas' disease. As with vertebrates, invertebrate animals also host a wealth of smaller parasites. Specialized fungi, for example, prey exclusively on insects. Thus for every animal added to an ecosystem, we can multiply the species diversity by this parasitism factor.

Parasites add more to an ecological system than just new names to the species list. The ecological interactions in which parasites participate are themselves a sort of resource that can influence the coexistence of species.

Conventionally, ecologists have considered resources like food, habitat, and breeding sites when studying the coexistence of species. But ecological interactions such as parasitism, pollination, herbivory, and seed dispersal can also mediate coexistence by promoting ecological specialization. How is it possible for six species of passion vine to share the same patch of rainforest? Some passion vines attract and support hummingbird pollinators; other species of *Passiflora* are pollinated by bees. The foliage of the different species varies in chemistry and in the types of caterpillars that are able to feed upon the leaves. The fruits range from small, grape-sized productions that are probably bird-dispersed to melon-sized fruits that attract relatively large mammals. The range of animal pollinators, fruit dispersers, and herbivores makes possible the evolution and coexistence of a rich set of *Passiflora* species. In turn, the diversity of the plants may mediate the coexistence of competing pollinators or herbivores.

Studying the process of plant-animal coevolution is a considerable challenge, since it occurs over an evolutionary time scale. At best, we know that such interactions lead to the generation of further diversity. Hence the ecologists' aphorism "diversity begets diversity" proves true, but only when the climate is constantly wet and warm enough to begin the initial green proliferation and promote its continuation. I try to keep this in mind whenever I have a face full of rain.

This weevil has been invaded and killed by one of a group of specialized fungi (*Cordyceps* spp.) that attack invertebrates. The fungus is just one of the multitude of parasites that contribute to the diversity found in rainforests.

Guanacaste
Forest reborn

Yellow cortez trees (*Tabebuia ochracea*) flowering prolifically on a Guanacaste hillside. Cortez is a "big bang" species in which all individuals bloom synchronously over a wide area. The trees burst into flower about four days after one of the infrequent rain showers that occur during the dry season. The flowers last only about four days, but usually there are several flowering episodes in the course of a dry season.

13

Guanacaste is a mass of gorgeous color during the dry season. Among the many spectacular flowering trees are pochote (*Pachira quinata*), above, and *Tabebuia rosea*, right—a pink-flowered relative of yellow cortez.

My first encounter with this forest felt both familiar and strange. There were howler monkeys howling and it sounded like I was in the rainforest. But it did not look that way. Sunlight brightened the forest floor. A thick layer of dead leaves crackled dryly underfoot as I walked through a gaunt, bare deciduous forest. I heard a commotion overhead and looked up to see a heavy lizard longer than my arm far out on a limb. It boasted a dramatic bluegray skin banded in black with a spiky dorsal fringe of protruding scales. Brilliant yellow flowers projected from its mouth. Having spent most of my time in tropical forests drenched with moisture, I found this dry deciduous forest in Guanacaste, Costa Rica, highly unusual. The trees were shorter and less diverse, and the climate obviously far more seasonal and severe than all the other tropical forests I had encountered.

Guanacaste is dry for half the year. The drought begins in December when the trade winds reach Costa Rica in full force. The winds come from the east across the Caribbean, but a wall of volcanic mountains confronts them before they hit Guanacaste province, a region lying along the northwest Pacific coast of Costa Rica. As the winds rise up over the mountains they drop their moisture and become dry; and, descending across the Guanacaste plains, they strip moisture from the landscape. By the time the New Year dawns, the clay soil is starting to crack. In response, the deciduous forests of Guanacaste throw off their leaves.

Dropping one's leaves is no trivial act for a plant. Leaves are the major photosynthetic organs allowing trees to synthesize sugars and to grow. They are costly to make. But a leaf costs more water than it is worth in the Guanacaste dry season. The water deficit developing in the soil and the strong, arid trade winds make it difficult to sustain the cost of leaky foliage. During photosynthesis leaves transpire water, which evaporates through the stomatal pores that open to allow carbon dioxide to enter the tissues. Large leaves are especially costly to the water balance. As a result, most large emergent trees are deciduous in Guanacaste. The few evergreen exceptions tend to be small and grow along river banks. Some understory trees take advantage of the increased light reaching the forest floor during the dry season. *Jaquinia pungens*, a shrub, actually sprouts leaves in the dry season—thin, leathery, needle-tipped leaves that probably are good at conserving water. A few trees such as *Bursera*, the gumbo limbo tree, shed their thin, red, flaking outer layer to reveal a green photosynthetic bark that continues to make some carbohydrates. But for the most part the forest stops growing and becomes as bare as a North American deciduous forest in December.

This might sound grim but it is only briefly so. A couple of months into the dry season, flower buds begin to swell. Then, day after day, here and there, entire tree crowns erupt en masse with bold blossoms. The result is as stunningly beautiful as—and a good deal more lively than—the autumnal displays of temperate deciduous forests. Mass flowering is probably an effective way to spread one's genes. It brings out a frenzy of pollinators busily harvesting the supply of pollen and nectar. Guanacaste has one of the largest documented bee faunas in the world—clouds of brilliant iridescent orchid bees, huge gold-

en *Centrus,* great black carpenter bees, tiny green halictid bees, and delicate banded leaf-cutting bees. The nectar and pollen draws them along with many sorts of flies, sphinx moths, butterflies, and hummingbirds.

Guanacaste is now a place of bright sunlight and openness. Much of the province has the aesthetic feel of the African savanna, except the big grazers are all cows and horses. In fact, the dominant grasses are African exotics. The trees in the "savannas," such as the Guanacaste that gives the province its name, have the classic umbrella spreading crowns characteristic of African savanna trees. This is pretty in a bucolic way, but it is not the original state of the landscape before humans arrived.

Guanacaste used to be wall-to-wall forest. In the 1960s and 1970s especially, the building of roads and bridges and the demand for beef in export markets made cattle ranching attrac-tive. Transportation to markets by truck became cheap and reliable. The World Bank and other lenders offered credit for those who wanted to turn forest into cattle pasture. Ranchers logged, burned, and plowed massive expanses of forest into pasture and seeded it with exotic African grasses. The dry forest that once extended from southern Mexico to Costa Rica was reduced to fragments covering a few percent of its former area.

When I first went to Guanacaste I was studying the social lives of tropical hornets. As a whole this group did well out of the extensive deforestation. The sunny scrubland and secondary forest that remained was wasp friendly. These areas had plenty of caterpillars and abundant nectar resources for the wasps to feed on. Never have I found more hornets per square foot. So I enjoyed my work in Guanacaste. Yet I never thought the region had much of a conservation future. Human-set fires and clearing

reduced the forest area every year. But of late, the conservation situation in Guanacaste has enjoyed a remarkable turnaround.

For the past three decades, the forest in the northern part of Guanacaste has been growing in extent, not shrinking. A remarkable coalition of conservationists has reclaimed a huge swath of Guanacaste in the form of the ACG (Area de Conservación Guanacaste; Guanacaste Conservation Area). Costa Rican conservationist Alvaro Ugalde—working with the tropical ecologist Dan Janzen, a man of legendary scientific accomplishment and profound energy—began building the system when Santa Rosa National Park was created. Ugalde was park director and Janzen was the scientific presence. From their partnership a much larger entity has evolved. They began to increase the size of the protected area not just by protecting the remaining old growth but by buying degraded land and regrowing the forest. This was and is an expensive proposition, because land already cleared and used for agriculture is expensive.

In the 1980s, I can remember shaking my head over hearing that Janzen was raising massive amounts of conservation money to buy cattle pasture. What was he thinking?

Much later the wisdom of this is readily apparent. The ACG now extends from the Pacific coast through the dry forest, up and over the cloud-forest-coated volcanoes down into the wet Atlantic lowlands. As such this swath is big enough to allow the flora and fauna to move appropriately as climate change occurs. The growing of the ACG came just in time. Not long ago, Guanacaste built an international airport that receives direct flights from the United States and elsewhere. This unleashed a rash of coastal zone hotel development. Land prices have soared even higher. But Janzen, an indefatigable fund raiser, has been able to continually acquire land for conservation in spite of the development pressure.

Recently I stood with Janzen on the midslope of one of the Guanacaste volcanoes overlooking his latest land acquisition for the ACG. We could look from the wet Atlantic to the dry Pacific watersheds, from the sweltering lowlands to the cool misty mountain tops. A more fortuitous arrangement for adjusting to climate change would have been hard to imagine. Clouds were forming on the tops of the volcanic cone and a rushing stream carried fresh water to the citrus farms below. I was seeing clearly now that a few determined prescient people can make, and indeed, have made—against all odds—a huge difference in the fate of tropical dry forest.

Tabebuia impetiginosa, left, is another of the spectacular Guanacaste trees that flowers in the dry season. The flowers of *Cassia grandis*, top right, here being visited by a honey bee (*Apis mellifera*), are unusual in providing pollen, rather than nectar, as a reward to pollinators. On the other hand, the flowers of the leguminous tree *Inga vera* produce abundant nectar at night for nocturnal pollinators, such as bats and hawk moths. Leftover nectar is eagerly taken the following morning by hummingbirds, in this case a green-breasted mango, bottom right.

Potential pollinators are not the only animals that are attracted to the nectar-rich flowers that enliven the dry forest. Mantled howler monkeys, left, eat many flowers, in this case those of the leguminous tree *Lochocarpus michelianus*. Pochote flowers (*Pachira quinata*) are particularly attractive. They open at night, and at dawn leftover nectar attracts variegated squirrels (*Sciurus variegatus*), top right, and a multitude of birds, including parrots, woodpeckers, and orioles. The spot-breasted oriole has even learned to pierce unopened buds to steal nectar, bottom right.

Many birds reach the southern limit of their range in the Guanacaste dry forest, including the turquoise-browed motmot, left, white-throated magpie-jay, above right, and rufous-naped wren, below right. They are among a group of species that are characteristic of the relatively arid region that extends along the Pacific coast from northern Mexico to Guanacaste.

The Guanacaste dry forest is an important wintering area for various migrants from North America, including most of the world's population of scissor-tailed flycatchers, right. During the day scissor-tailed flycatchers forage alone or in small groups, but in the evening hundreds of birds gather in communal roosts. Guanacaste is also an important wintering area for ruby-throated hummingbirds. This molting male, left, is feeding at the flowers of the leguminous tree *Gliricidia sepium*.

As well as encompassing beautiful dry forest, Palo Verde National Park protects the important wetlands found along the lower reaches of the Tempisque and Bebedero rivers. These wetlands provide wintering and breeding habitat for huge numbers of waterbirds, including egrets and spoonbills, top left, rare jabirus, bottom left, and purple gallinules, right.

Frogs
Life history strategies in rainforest amphibians

When two male poison dart frogs stand upright, their arms wrapped around each other, their heads thrown back, calling out as they strain, stagger, and wrestle on the forest floor, we are treated to an earnest display of machismo. Their skin is slick, their reddish yellow bellies are rotund, and their blue legs are bowed, causing a friend to liken them to sumo wrestlers in blue jeans.

One might say that the description of male *Dendrobates pumilio* frogs competing for breeding territories is anthropomorphic. I would agree. Let me immediately confess that my thoughts on frogs are colored by empathy. Most naturalists feel the same way about frogs, perhaps because members of the order Anura—the "tailless ones"—are easy animals with which to identify. The great evolutionary biologists J. B. S. Haldane and Julian Huxley long ago observed: "The statement that frogs resemble men in any important degree may perhaps raise a smile. It is nevertheless true. We can recognize in the frog a great many parts that exist in ourselves, arranged, moreover, in the same way." That the frog is an organism that reminds us of ourselves may explain why so many cultures have myths featuring the conversion of frogs into princes, sorcerers, and other sorts of humans. But more than simple anatomical kinship, it is also a question of attitude that makes frogs endearing.

Frogs, especially the tree frogs so common in rainforests, have a way of facing you with a goggle-eyed gaze that is disconcertingly humanoid. Their huge wraparound mouths, while perhaps not actually resembling a smile, are certainly not frowning. Sitting hunched up as though in anticipation, they assume the posture and calm demeanor of patient listeners ready to participate in conversation.

Who cannot feel enchantment upon encountering the delicate translucence of a glass frog perched on a leaf, upon hearing the whooping entreaty of a pond full of male smoky jungle frogs (*Leptodactylus pentadactylus*) on a warm tropical evening, or upon feeling the splayed sucker toes of a tree frog gently grasping one's skin? Our emotional responses to these appealing features of frogs are not irrelevant. The art of natural history lies in allowing such personal reactions to organisms to lead us into their biology.

Unlike most vertebrates, frogs tend to sit quietly rather than to panic and flee when you approach. That makes them an easy animal with which to make contact. Their moist skin has a tactile appeal and is tastefully patterned in perfect rainforest attire. And because they are virtually harmless, most species can be picked up with impunity; none that I know of stink up your hand the way many snakes and turtles do. Only a few of them bite with any conviction, and the small wounds they inflict are probably worth the novelty of being one of a handful of people who can claim to have been bitten by a frog. Their sometimes potent defensive toxins are never injected. The giant toad *Bufo marinus* can squirt out a dilute stream of irritating toxin from its parotid glands, although to its credit, it does this more often to dogs than to humans. A few species, such as *Leptodactylus pentadactylus* and *Phrynohyas venulosa*, have a skin secretion that makes your fingers tingle or even burn if it gets into a wound; the exudates of certain species will induce vomiting if rubbed on your forearms (something various Guyanese tribes in search of a cathartic purification used to do willingly). Generally, however, for a frog to do you real damage, you have to chew it.

The red-eyed leaf frog (*Agalychnis callidryas*) is one of the gaudiest and most photographed frogs in the world.

The aptly named reticulated glass frog (*Hyalinobatrachium valerioi*), top, is among the most beautiful and delicate of its kind. Note the bones and blood vessels that are visible through its transparent skin.

When threatened, the bizarre horned frog (*Hemiphractus* sp.), bottom, opens its enormous mouth, exposing its pink tongue. Given the chance it also bites tenaciously, inflicting small punctures with the sharp, toothlike spikes that tip its lower jaw.

Even a cursory examination of these particular features of rainforest frogs reveals that two themes, moisture and predation pressure, explain the conspicuous and attractive aspects of their anatomy and behavior. The humid rainforest microclimate has a liberating effect on frogs. A curious limitation of the physiology of these amphibians is a need for constantly high humidity. Yet in spite of their apparent affinity for the stuff, frogs never actually drink water. Instead, they drink and breathe through their skin. Water and respiratory gases pass freely back and forth across this huge membrane. In open or dry areas, frogs tend to stay in the water. But in rainforests, frogs sit openly on leaves. Temperate-zone frogs hop about using the same, paired frog-kick that jets them in bursts through the water. In rainforests, frogs with long, stretched-out limbs and digits, sometimes with webbed skin, climb arm over arm to their destination. The eyes are positioned forward on the head for better depth perception. The spider monkeys and flying squirrels of the amphibia, they are arboreal climbers that sometimes leap out into space and glide from one tree to another. By comparison, temperate-zone frogs seem a squat and lumpish lot.

The huddled posture that arboreal frogs typically adopt by tucking their limbs under their bodies is a water-conservation strategy that reduces evaporation from their surface area during dry times; it may also reduce heat loss. At room temperature and 100 percent humidity, a frog will lose only 20 percent of its metabolic heat through evaporative cooling; but if the humidity drops to only 94 percent, the heat lost through evaporation will equal all the heat generated by the frog's metabolism. A frog stretched out and placed in direct sun would wither away in no time; even the prodigiously large *Bufo marinus*, a five-pin-bowling-ball-sized toad that can reach a weight of 2.6 pounds (1.2 kg) and has a leathery, warty hide, is highly susceptible to water loss. At 80 percent humidity, an individual without water can become lethally dehydrated in twenty-four hours. Most frogs were made for warm, drizzly nights.

Access to higher nighttime humidity is one important benefit of being nocturnally active. But being active by night also helps the frog to avoid the legions of predators that are only too ready to make a meal of it. Fish have probably been eating frogs since ancestral frogs and fish began to diverge evolutionarily. Several species of snakes have evolved into specialized hunters of adult frogs, and some bats have developed a sonar and hearing system that enables them to swoop down and snag calling males. Coatimundis, opossums—indeed, most carnivorous mammals—include frogs in their diet, as do many birds such as hawks, herons, rails, muscovy ducks, and motmots. Crabs, spiders, water bugs, and the larvae of some beetles and flies also attack frogs successfully. There are even frogs that specialize in eating other frogs. And although certain tadpoles may be capable of chemical defense, most can be slurped down expeditiously. Much of the radiation of rainforest frogs into new niches seems to be driven by these varied predation pressures.

The significance of predation on the life history of frogs is evident not only in their anatomy but also in their sophisticated reproductive behavior. The battle of the male *Dendrobates pumilio*, performed so openly in broad daylight, on dry land, and in such bold

attire, might strike most naturalists as unusual. The scene arouses an initial interest similar to that evoked by witnessing a barroom brawl. But it is not long before we start to wonder exactly why the frogs are fighting on the forest floor, so far from any river or pond. What sort of payoff do they receive for their efforts?

The reproductive and parental rituals of *Dendrobates* are among the most elaborate in nature. The male defends areas of leaf litter in a patch of forest where there are also water-filled bromeliads that provide a habitat for the tadpoles. He advertises with a buzzy, chirping call that attracts females. When a female approaches, the territorial male hops to a leaf and deposits a squirt of sperm, upon which the female lays three to ten relatively large eggs. The male then broods the eggs right on the forest floor. After about two weeks, the eggs hatch into tadpoles that wriggle up onto the back of the female and adhere with the aid of their mucous coating and sucking mouths. The adult frogs then carry and distribute the tadpoles among the territory's water-filled bro-

The conspicuous black and blue colors of this Suriname endemic, the blue poison dart frog (*Dendrobates azureus*), signal the presence of complex and poisonous alkaloids in the skin secretions that protect it against most predators. The secretions of some poison dart frogs are so toxic that they are used by rainforest tribes to poison the tips of their blowgun darts.

meliads. The bromeliads contain some food for the tadpoles, but to ensure an adequate supply, the tadpoles are usually dispersed one per plant. More remarkably, the female repeatedly visits the plants to lay unfertilized eggs in each one. The tadpoles puncture the eggs and suck out their yolky contents.

Territory-holding male *Dendrobates* are evidently a limited resource and one that females court actively; studies of breeding areas have found that female adults usually outnumber males. In species where the male broods eggs or carries tadpoles, the

This rear-fanged halloween snake (*Urotheca euryzona*), left, just one of many snakes that specialize in a diet of frogs, is swallowing a rain frog (*Eleutherodactylus noblei*).

Male strawberry poison dart frogs (*Dendrobates pumilio*), right, wrestle on the forest floor for control over territory; their bold colors advertise their toxicity to would-be predators.

female takes a particularly aggressive role in courtship. In the case of *Dendrobates auratus*, a beautiful species with blue-green, turquoise, and dark markings, the female makes an attempt to gain a male's attention by leaping on his back and poking him with her forelimbs.

An adult *Dendrobates* is freed somewhat from the threat of predation by virtue of its alkaloid-impregnated skin, although specialized predators such as *Liophis* snakes will eat even the most toxic frogs, including *Dendrobates*. But this relative immunity is only one factor that allows *Dendrobates* to wrestle and court by day.

The second significant aspect of *Dendrobates* breeding is that much of it takes place on land. The humid rainforest microclimate and the many small, moist havens found there explain much of the reproductive variety frogs achieve in tropical rainforests. Herpetologist Martha Crump found eighty-one species of frogs in one patch of Ecuadoran rainforest. Ecuador, incidentally, a tiny but fantastically varied country, has some three hundred frog species. By comparison, Great Britain has but three, and the entire United States, with all its lakes, rivers, and wetlands, has only eighty species.

The low anuran diversity in North America is initially surprising; a temperate-zone naturalist might reasonably expect lakes, ponds, and marshes to be the most popular haunts of frogs. It is

not true. Preferred habitats are, in fact, those harboring the fewest predators. The frog diversity in the main Amazonian rivers, for example, is as low as the fish diversity is great. Instead, most frogs occur in the forest proper.

A tropical rainforest offers a variety of habitats that no pond, lake, or river can match. It is replete with small temporary ponds, such as water-filled bromeliads, and crotches and holes in trees. The latter are apparently defended by the male of the giant tree frog *Hyla miliaria*, which has a stout thumb spine that it probably jabs in the face of an intruding rival. Such elevated breeding habitats are simply not available to frogs outside of tropical rainforests.

The breeding strategies of rainforest frogs are best appreciated when compared with those of their northern relatives. Nearly every temperate-zone frog has the same basic life history. When the spring thaw arrives, croaking, trilling, and *chugarrumming* calls go out from the males. In response, females issue masses of spawn into pond and marsh shallows. Males fertilize thousands of eggs, then abandon them to their fate. Most eggs are eaten; some become tadpoles. The major procedural difference among species is in the timing. Wood frogs stage a mass orgiastic event in ice water, while bullfrogs prefer warm water. But 90 percent of temperate-zone species simply lay their eggs in ponds. Herpetologists such as William Duellman note that in all

of North America, there are only four different modes of frog reproduction. By contrast, Duellman recognizes fourteen reproductive behaviors in tropical South America, eleven of which occur in a single rainforest locality.

While the ancestral breeding habitat of all frogs is thought to have been standing bodies of water like ponds and marshes, such conventional environments are not necessary for rainforest frogs; they have spread into breeding habitats that are more terrestrial and arboreal. Rainforests are often wet enough for frogs to use a mere leaf as an egg-laying site. Many rainforest frogs, including species of the genera *Phyllomedusa, Agalychnis, Hyalinobatrachium,* and *Hyla,* place their eggs on vegetation that grows above water. Upon hatching, the tadpoles drop down into the water. In some species of *Colostethus,* the adult will carry the adherent tadpoles to running water after they hatch.

In various leptodactylid frogs such as *Leptodactylus* and *Physalaemus pustulosus,* the adults produce a nest of foam. Typi-

cally, the male takes hold of the female from behind and adds his sperm to the mass of eggs and jelly she releases. The male whips the mass by kicking his hind legs back and forth until he creates a protective froth around the eggs.

Male egg guarding is well developed in some species of glass frogs. The male *Hyalinobatrachium* often sits on or beside the jellylike egg mass to attend it. This egg guarding serves two purposes: first, it keeps away flies, wasps, and other insects that might feed on the eggs (although what the frog does when a specialized frog-egg-eating snake such as *Leptodeira* comes along is not known); second, it regulates moisture.

Unlike the eggs of birds and reptiles, frog eggs have no membrane for retaining moisture and so dry out rapidly. Rainforest frogs have several ways of preventing this, even if their eggs are laid on the forest floor or on vegetation. In the genus *Eleutherodactylus,* the eggs absorb water osmotically from the skin of the brooding adult. In many species, the adult frog carries water

An adult red-backed poison dart frog (*Dendrobates reticulatus*), left, carrying tadpoles to water.

The eggs of rain frogs (*Eleutherodactylus* spp.), right, are laid in damp leaf litter rather than water. There the embryos undergo direct development, metamorphosing completely into froglets within the eggs.

to the eggs. The female *Agalychnis callidryas*, the world's most garishly pigmented frog, lays her eggs on leaves with an adherent male locked in a mate-guarding grip on her back. With the male still clamped on, the female then descends into a pool and absorbs water through her skin. Because a frog's blood is saltier than rainwater, osmotic pressure and the frog's water-permeable skin allow it to absorb into the circulatory system a great deal of water, which eventually finds its way into the bladder. Normally, that excess water is excreted as dilute urine; fully aquatic frogs such as *Pipa pipa* urinate continuously. (One of the perverse little experiments that have been performed on frogs—usually on the unfortunate leopard frog *Rana pipiens*—is to tie the cloaca shut, thereby preventing urination; the sealed-off frog placed in a beaker of water soon swells up like a balloon.) The female *Agalychnis* turns this physiological feature to her own advantage and acts as a watering can to moisten her eggs soon after laying, so that they have enough water to complete their development.

A common life-history alternative to all these strategies is known as direct development. Highly evolved in tropical rainforests and cloud forests, the process completely bypasses the vulnerable tadpole stage. Instead, the embryo grows into a froglet inside the egg itself. One expects such development of snakes, turtles, and birds, which have well-developed eggshells and protective membranes; but those who have grown up watching jars of gelatinous frog spawn metamorphose into tadpoles may find it difficult to believe. However, it has advantages. Typically, the eggs of direct developers are large and laid not in water but on the forest floor in some humid, protected spot. No doubt, rainforest frogs have evolved to direct development for a variety of reasons, but several benefits are clear. Rather than the tadpole being responsible for gathering the food that will enable it to become a frog, as is the case with pond breeders, the embryo in direct-development reproduction is provided with a huge store of food in the egg mass. Often, the female simply lays the eggs and leaves them on the ground, which reduces the exposure of the immature stages to aquatic predators while allowing the mother to remain mobile to forage for food and lay more eggs.

Some frogs in the genus *Eleutherodactylus* even retain their eggs within their bodies until tiny but complete frogs hatch. The disadvantage is reduced fecundity, the classic trade-off between quantity and quality. Greater parental investment in each offspring means reduced infant mortality, but frogs that employ direct development often have clutches of less than a dozen eggs, while pond breeders may lay thousands. Live birth is comparable, in effect, to another strategy: some frogs avoid egg desiccation and predation by carrying their eggs and tadpoles embedded in their backs. *Gastrotheca* males use their feet to collect the eggs laid by the female; after fertilizing them, the male shoves the eggs into a pouch on the female's back. In some species, the eggs develop all the way to the froglet stage, while in others, such as the pygmy marsupial frog (*Flectonotus pygmaeus*), the tadpoles are released at an advanced stage into tank bromeliads.

A pair of reticulated glass frogs (*Hyalinobatrachium valerioi*), left, tends two clutches of eggs laid on a leaf overhanging a forest stream. They make sure that the eggs do not dry out and guard them against egg parasites and small predatory insects.

The huge throat sac of this calling male Brazilian tree frog (*Hyla* sp.), right, is a resonating chamber. It amplifies a mating call designed to attract females and to repel male rivals.

This reproductive diversity appears to be the key feature that enables eighty or more species to inhabit the same patch of forest. However, the variety in breeding and development strategies stands in marked contrast to the adult frog's rather unremarkable feeding specializations. The big mouth that many frogs have is a giveaway; it is the hallmark of a sit-and-wait predator prepared to maximize its intake.

There are few small-mouthed frogs. Specialized fossorial feeders on termites, such as the burrowing toad (*Rhinophrynus dorsalis*), the *Dendrobates*, and other small frogs that eat mainly ants and small litter insects, all have relatively small mouths and heads. But most frogs are big-headed and big-mouthed generalists. They engulf just about anything that comes their way. The smoky jungle frog, for example, eats frogs almost as large as itself; it even eats 2-foot-long (0.5 m) snakes. The bizarre *Ceratophrys* has taken this approach to the extreme and is known to swallow rodents whole. Some species sit half-buried in the leaf litter like a living pitfall trap and may even wiggle their protruding toes to attract another curious frog or an insect-eating lizard. What a frog's stomach contains reflects where it lives and breeds rather than a selectivity in diet.

A huge head and mouth also serve frogs in good stead for singing. For nocturnal animals dispersed high and low in the forest, sound is clearly the signal of choice—yet another feature that connects frogs with humans. While fish, salamanders, snakes, and turtles are an inarticulate lot, restricted to grunting and hissing, frogs share with birds a sensory channel upon which humans can eavesdrop. Some calls advertise, some are territorial and agonistic. Some songs are based on one note, others on clusters of notes. A number of frog species sing in synchronized choruses that may attract females while making it difficult for predators to home in on a specific target.

Frogs generate sound by means of inflatable air sacs, located under and alongside the mouth or body, that act as resonating chambers when air from the lungs and huge mouth cavity is blown across the vocal cords. Because of all their volume—sometimes as much as 100 decibels—it is often easier to hear rainforest frogs than to see them. A thumbnail-sized species of *Eleutherodactylus* known as the tink frog is particularly frustrating; its call is both loud and pervasive. As daylight fades in the cloud forest, a mounting chorus of *tink, tink, tink*—a penetrating staccato call—rings all around you. But try to find the callers. You bend your head this way and that, peering and trying to discern the nearest source. If you are absolutely still, one may start to call right beside you; as you inch toward it, however, the hidden caller becomes silent. The vociferous but tiny tink frog is rarely seen except by accident. This secretive aspect of frogs is sometimes well developed because various

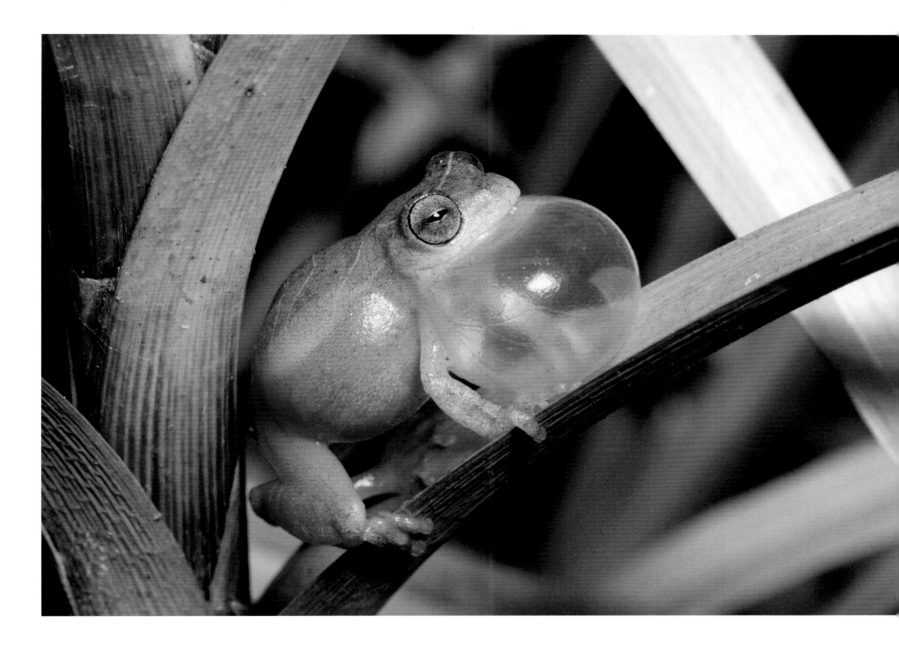

predators—bats, caimans, mammals, and other frogs, especially the large engulfers such as *Bufo marinus* and *Leptodactylus pentadactylus*—are alert to frog calls.

The panoply of frog calls enlivens the rainforest during its darkest, dampest moments. On a drizzling, dripping-wet evening, you will almost certainly hear them at their most enthusiastic. On a ridgetop far from any pond or stream, there will be frogs of some sort; their most reliable characteristic is their ubiquity. Tree frogs will sit openly on the leaves of the shrubbery. You can stare into their large, gold-rimmed eyes without stooping, and they may make a chameleonlike change of color in the light of your headlamp. You will find frogs clinging to tree trunks like bits of wet, rubbery lichen. As you sweep your headlamp along the trail, many a dull brown frog and sometimes a bold black, yellow, and red *Atelopus* toad can be seen in the leaf litter, while far overhead in the treetops, a marsupial frog makes a barking sound.

The last time I went for a walk in a tropical forest, I was lucky. While inspecting a mass of blue flowers, I discovered that it held a tink frog. It perched cooperatively on my finger for a minute as I inspected it—a tiny, perfect bit of a frog; then an impressive two-yard leap carried it back into obscurity. I stood there for a few minutes, appreciating once more the particular pleasure frogs can provide. Having made their escape from the confinements of ponds and rivers, radiating into all the strata of the forest, rainforest frogs are a kind of zoological equivalent of epiphytic plants. They are an appropriate emblem of tropical rainforests, for they owe their rich diversity to the hallmark of that habitat. Freedom for frogs comes with the rain.

Rarity

Why rare species are
common in the tropics

We were following the Peñas Blancas River down to a point below where it dropped nearly 1,000 feet (300 m) into a steep canyon. Above the drop, the river ran clear and fast over rounded boulders. The upper river had no fish but was populated instead by purple crabs and caddis fly larvae and was patrolled by dippers and torrent tyrannulets, birds that prefer cold, moving water. Not far below the gorge, the river grew silty and warm, beginning its sprawling entry into the Atlantic lowlands. Our destination was the transition zone between the upland montane rainforest and the lowlands, a place where we hoped to see a bird known as the keel-billed motmot. Michael Fogden had described the bird as rare, and I believed him; the mere possibility of sighting it had induced him to hike for hours up and down interminably long ridges, along an often muddy trail, sometimes wading through rivers. No one else I knew had ever seen the bird. In fact, several of the birders I had met in Costa Rica seemed not to know of its existence. The keel-billed motmot was rare, and I wanted to see the bird for that reason alone.

Setting out, we had searched for an old game track, a thin mud line sketched by peccaries' hooves and hunters' boots that reputedly traced a route from the top of the ridge down to the river. The trail began well enough, threading its way through the long, graceful trunks of chonta palms (*Bactris* spp.), along a breezy but gently sloping ridge. The sides of the ridge soon fell away. We stopped to peer cautiously over the edge at a waterfall

Although the mountain lion (*Felis concolor*) is very widely distributed geographically, it exists, like most cats, at low densities. Like other predators that feed near the end of the food chain, it survives by hunting for mammals both large and small, such as deer, agoutis, and rats.

spraying over a cove-shaped cliff, the sort of spot beloved by swifts as a breeding site and perhaps the birthplace of the legions of white-collared, chestnut-collared, and white-chinned swifts that swept the cloud-hung sky above the valley. Then the trail began to dwindle away. Our ridge narrowed to a 3-foot-wide (1 m) strip of rocks, moss, and, at one point, air—one of those places where the division between solid earth and the atmosphere is far from clear. The ridge expanded at a small promontory before falling steeply and dissolving into a jumble of boulders and forest.

The prospect was not promising, and it looked worse after we had crawled down the first 165 feet (50 m). We were on the point of writing off the attempt as a failure, when Michael looked up with widened eyes. Pointing out a modest bird perched on a liana just overhead, he instructed me to keep my eye on it as he scrambled higher for a better look. I spotted a companion bird sitting nearby and kept them in view with no appreciation of the privilege of such a sight. After a minute, Michael announced that there was no doubt about it—we were watching perhaps the rarest bird in all of Costa Rica, not the keel-billed motmot but an oddity known to a select few as the lanceolated monklet.

A mere handful of bird, the lanceolated monklet was clearly a member of the puffbird family. It had the characteristic rictal bristles around its bill, a stub tail, and a rotund body that seemed almost inflated. Its plumage was subdued but nicely lanceolated, streaked with tracings and dabs of buff-brown on white.

Compared with a motmot (or, for that matter, many other animals and birds), the lanceolated monklet was hardly impressive. But it was special because it was scarce in the most basic sense: hardly anyone had ever seen one. When I returned home, I read what I could find on this bird in Ridgely's *A Guide to the Birds of Panama* and was surprised to learn that there seemed

Sitting on its nest, the relatively rare sunbittern, left, displays its remarkable "eyespots." The sunbittern hunts and nests only along the margins of rivers and lakes in tropical forests, each breeding pair ranging over a wide area.

Montane cloud forests and rainforests like those at Monteverde, Costa Rica, right, often harbor rare, endemic species—organisms that are found nowhere else. Alteration of a small area of habitat can cause their extinction.

to have been only three sightings in all of Panama during the twentieth century. Michael informed me that our sighting (which was his second) was only the third for all of Costa Rica—this in a country which swarms with bird watchers visiting a great array of national parks and preserves. That gave the bird more of a mystique than its appearance alone might evoke.

Most naturalists share an interest in rarity. Although humans value rarity per se—witness the prices of trinkets and commodities whose only merit is their scarcity—there are more specific reasons for our fascination with rarity in rainforests. There is a commonness to rarity there. That sounds contradictory, but tropical forests are indeed full of species represented by small numbers of individuals in any given spot, the inevitable consequence of high species diversity. Rare species also arouse interest for a practical reason: they are sensitive indicators of change. To be rare is to flirt with extinction.

Before we can understand rarity, we have to understand what we mean by the word. "Uncommon" will not do as a definition. The lanceolated monklet occurs all the way from Costa Rica down through Peru. The total population size of this widely distributed species may amount to many thousands of individuals. While the naturalist considers the species to be rare in terms of population density, the biogeographer might consider it to be common in terms of geographic range and total numbers.

Thus the word "rare" may have many ecological meanings. Happily, plant ecologist Deborah Rabinowitz has given us a neat, logical framework for articulating what we mean by rarity. Rabinowitz suggests that we consider three things about a species: how great its geographic range is, how restricted its habitat choice is, and how abundant it is in its habitat. These criteria give us an objective way to analyze what we mean by rare.

Only one type of rarity has well-understood ecological causes: the low-density rarity typical of big, fierce animals. Animals such as carnivorous cats that feed at the end of food chains are forced to be rare for thermodynamic reasons. While plants harvest but a small fraction of the light energy that hits the Earth's surface—some 2 to 4 percent—the animals eating those plants convert an even smaller percentage of that plant biomass into animal biomass. (Estimates suggest that only about 0.1 percent may be converted into animal form.) And carnivores that feed on those animals convert a smaller percentage again. The margay, a spotted cat whose primary prey is birds, can never be very abundant. The cat that eats the bird that ate the insects that ate the plants is at the low-density limit set by the second law of thermodynamics: every transformation of matter results in a loss of energy. Carnivores dependent on food derived from three or four previous transformations in the food chain simply have less food available to them in a given area than do herbivores.

Predator species such as margays live at low densities within a broad geographic distribution. In other words, there are few individuals in an area, but the species is spread over a large mass of land. Consider the lanceolated monklet. Hardly ever seen, it may either be secretive, be an extreme habitat specialist, or exist at very low densities. But is it rare? The monklet shares the attribute of a wide geographic distribution with the margay, the jaguar, the giant otter, and the harpy eagle, animals conventionally considered to be the rarest species in the tropical forest.

On the other hand, the thermodynamic argument that explains why big, fierce animals are rare cannot be applied to the lanceolated monklet or to the keel-billed motmot. Monklets and keel-billed motmots feed much lower in the trophic pyramid and are not rare because of lack of food availability the way that cats are. Nor would one expect many plants, save the few carnivorous species, to show this pattern of rarity, since they are at the bottom of the food chain. And indeed, the British flora that Rabinowitz studied revealed that such rarity—wide habitat choice and great geographic range but low density—is not a common plant-distribution pattern.

The alternative to the trophic-level account of rarity is ecological specialization. A species might be rare because it has evolved a restricted set of ecological requirements such as a specialized diet or habitat. The lanceolated monklet could have an uncommon nesting site or habitat, perhaps the mud-packed roots of windthrown trees on mountain slopes.

Along the Peñas Blancas River, for example, we had seen sunbitterns wading. They are large birds of a strangely hybrid construction, not unlike a combination of a heron, a bittern, and a grebe. Sunbitterns have a dramatic display that consists of lifting and spreading their wings to reveal sunburst-colored feathers arranged in two fantastic giant "eyespots." On the whole river, there are probably only a handful of breeding pairs. In part, this is because the birds are upper-level predators that eat crabs, frogs, lizards, and predatory insects such as hellgrammites—prey that are themselves secondary consumers. But in addition, sunbitterns may be uncommon because they are specialized with respect to both habitat and breeding sites. In Central America, sunbitterns prefer fast-flowing, clear-water rivers. They rely on trees overhanging the river as sites for their bowl-shaped nests of leaves, moss, and mud. Were it not for their dependence on a special habitat—the narrow strip between rainforest and permanent, clear-moving waters—sunbitterns might well be a more common sight.

The same is true for many rare plants. Botanical rarity is usually the result of restricted habitat choice. When Rabinowitz and her botanical colleagues analyzed the British flora for rare forms, they found that specialized habitat choice accounts for the greatest proportion of rare species: nearly one-third of the rare British plants had coastal distributions. Few tropical ecologists have looked at this trend, although Robin Foster and Steve Hubbell have laboriously mapped tree locations and analyzed patterns of commonness and rarity in Panamanian trees. About half of the rare trees were habitat specialists in large light gaps, swamps, streams, and ravines. A habitat type such as ravine forest or large light gap may have a great geographic distribution, but the species that specialize in such places are sparsely distributed in thin strips and small flecks across the continent.

Rabinowitz found that the second most common form of rarity was the geographically restricted endemic, that is, a species which is confined to a small geographic range. In the tropics, an increasing proportion of rarity is accounted for by these limited geographic distributions. So-called endemic species can be common locally, but because they are found only in limited geographic ranges, they are considered rare. And the narrowness of their distribution is sometimes inexplicably arbitrary.

Leading down the Peñas Blancas River Valley, in Costa Rica, is a swath of cloud forest and elfin woodland, a moss-draped, gnarly woodland raked and stunted by the wind and bogged deep in accumulated humus, peat, and debris. It is a fog- and rain-catching device par excellence, and the water harvested from the cumulus clouds carried on the trade winds eventually becomes the crystal-clear Peñas Blancas River. In an especially wet and windy section of this woodland, there once was a brilliant golden toad (*Bufo periglenes*), which in its masculine form was surely the most flamboyant toad on Earth. It bred only in the temporary pools of water that form on the Continental Divide after the first heavy Easter rains. During these explosive breeding episodes, the toad appeared to be abundant; the pools fairly swarmed with them. But in terms of geography and total population, this toad was surely one of the rarest of organisms. All of its orange-pigmented glory was contained in perhaps less than half a square mile (1 km²) of soggy mountain ridge; it existed nowhere else on the planet. This toad, which is likely now extinct, was a classic example of endemic rarity.

A male bare-necked umbrellabird on its display perch in the Monteverde Cloud Forest Preserve. This umbrellabird breeds in very wet, mid-elevation forests, a zone that harbors many rare species with limited distributions.

The empress brilliant, top left, is restricted to the Chocó rainforest region of western Colombia and Ecuador. It is one of the wettest areas in the world, and it supports numerous rare plants and animals with restricted ranges.

The magenta-throated woodstar, bottom right, here feeding at blueberry flowers (*Gonocalyx* sp.), is a rare and local species of the highlands of Costa Rica and western Panama. For four months of the year, it disappears from its breeding grounds on the Pacific slope of the mountains. Although it is not known exactly where it goes, it probably migrates to remote areas of forest on the Caribbean slope.

The vulnerability of such endemic species to even minor habitat modification is striking. The Monteverde Cloud Forest Preserve had to be created to save the golden toad from a proposed dairy farm that would have converted its entire range into pasture. The creation of a single farm would have cast this unique toad off its mountain haunt into that abyss of extinction from which no creature can ever return. In fact, in spite of this protection, the golden toad is now almost certainly extinct. Even after extensive searching by biologists, no golden toads have been seen since 1989. The extinction of the golden toad (and many other amphibians) has probably been caused by outbreaks of a pathogenic fungus promoted and encouraged by global warming.

Geographically restricted endemics like the golden toad are more at risk than the big, fierce rarities that not only have charisma and anthropomorphic appeal on their side but also are buffered against extinction by their broad geographic range. The relationship between endemism, rarity, and extinction is statistically clear-cut. The laws of probability dictate that chance events and fluctuations will extinguish populations at a rate that is inversely proportional to their size and geographic distribution.

If mass extinctions through human interference are to be avoided, it is necessary to map and protect centers of endemism. These centers are not all known, but it is clear that they manifest very particular features. Tropical mountaintops, for example, are like islands: they favor the creation of new species because their physical isolation separates populations from a previously widespread gene pool. Physiological specialization to the cool, damp environment makes subsequent dispersal and interbreeding with other distant, high-altitude populations difficult because they are set apart by hot lowland areas. The resulting local population on the mountaintop may gradually become genetically adapted to a restricted area; perhaps it diverges from the large ancestral population simply through the chance circumstances that are an inevitable part of the life history of such populations.

In some areas, clusters of endemic species make up a large fraction of the region's flora and fauna. In Venezuela and the Guianas, for example, the tops of the tepui mountains—isolated sandstone plugs that stand out above the Guiana shield—have endemism rates as high as 54 percent. More than half the plants on top of a tepui will be found there and nowhere else. These endemics combine to make up several thousand of the estimated ten thousand plant species found in the region. In other words, localized endemism contributes a large proportion of the area's total species count. In such regions, therefore, a significant proportion of the species is inherently rare. Preserving and protecting just one mountaintop protects only a fraction of the species of the mountain countries of Central and South America. This pattern of endemic rarity dictates that a larger amount of habitat must be preserved than in temperate areas, where endemism is less common.

Botanist Al Gentry had the fortune and the anguish of studying a remarkable concentration of endemic plants on the Centinela Ridge in the western foothills of the Ecuadoran Andes before the area was cleared for cattle pasture. The ridge contained an 8-square-mile (20 km²) stand of cloud forest. In it, Gentry found thirty-eight endemic plants—thirty-eight species that occur no-

The golden toad (*Bufo periglenes*) was a rare species found only along a short stretch of mountain ridge in Costa Rica. The brilliant golden-orange males and mottled females used to congregate to breed in pools left by the first spring rains. However, no mating aggregations have been found for more than twenty years (and no individual since 1989), and the golden toad is now presumed extinct. Species with tiny ranges are very vulnerable to extinction.

A scaled antpitta at its nest. Antpittas and other birds of the forest understory do not disperse across open country. As forest becomes fragmented, they quickly disappear from the smaller patches.

where else on Earth—a high percentage of which had intensely pigmented, almost black leaves. Now, Centinela Ridge is stubble and cows. All that remains of the endemics are a few dry, pressed specimens in herbarium cabinets.

Near Centinela Ridge is the forest at the Palenque River. With almost six hundred species per half square mile (1 km²), it probably has the highest recorded plant diversity in the world; it, too, is being isolated and eroded. The trashing of the Palenque River area has taken place recently, for reasons and at a rate that typify the erosion of tropical diversity. When I first visited the Palenque River in 1974, the new road—a former mule track from Quito and the highlands to Guayaquil and the coast—had been upgraded into a wide, graveled, all-weather conduit to the western lowlands. The nearest town of any size to Palenque was Santo Domingo de los Colorados. The boom was on, but the town was still commonly visited by Colorado Indians, wearing their skirts of black and white concentric rings and their hair slicked down into a red helmet fashioned from a dense slather of achiote paste. The agricultural expansion made possible by better road access was fueled by a worldwide hunger for edible oils and timber. The foothills and alluvial plain, with their great forests of hardwood, their balsa along the rivers, and their soils well suited for oil-palm plantations, were up for grabs.

Even in 1974, large areas right around the biological station were being cleared, although plenty of habitat still remained. Looking back east over the river, you could see endless stretches of unbroken forest on the serrated ridges and rolling Andean foothills. The river ran clear and silt-free. In the dry season, you could pole a balsa raft upstream and then snorkel back downstream, peering into clear pools that were patrolled by pugnacious orange-bellied cichlid fish. You could roll over to look at sungrebes and kingfishers perched on the tree limbs overhanging the river. Birders knew Palenque as one of the best spots in Latin America to see such exotica as the harpy eagle. The biological station's list of primary-forest birds recorded about 170 species, and there were dozens of open-habitat and riparian species besides, making a grand total of 336 species, which represents about a third the total diversity of North America. All of these managed to survive in a patch of forest only 412 acres (167 hectares) in area.

Palenque has become just that—an island of forest in a desolation of oil palm and pasture. The entire Santo Domingo area has been flooded with half a million people, and the forest has been completely swept from the foothills and ridges, a transformation of a landscape so vast that it would seem impossible to anyone who had not seen it happen. A few of the most valuable trees, including an endemic laurel that was the premier lumber species, are now known to exist only as a handful of individuals in the remaining Palenque forest.

The avifauna and mammalian fauna have likewise been severely depleted. Ornithologist Charles Leck compared the avifauna records of 1973 and 1978. In five years, 26 percent of the forest birds had disappeared. Of the 170 species of forest birds, Leck found no evidence of 19 species, 25 had not been seen in three years, and 15 had precariously low populations. The species that had become extinct were those that are typically rare; large

birds of prey and highly specialized birds, such as antbirds, were the first to vanish. Edibles like guans, toucans, and parrots were disappearing because of poaching pressure. Among the mammals, the big predators—the puma, ocelot, tayra, and grison weasel—had disappeared.

The conclusions are not surprising, nor are they new: both predatory mammals and ecologically specialized birds are very vulnerable to isolation. In fact, it is not necessary to deforest an area completely to cause extinction; simply decreasing the patch will do the job, even on large islands such as Panama's 6-square-mile (15 km²) Barro Colorado Island. Edwin Willis has recorded the island's loss of some forty-five bird species. They include the biggest raptor, the harpy eagle; the biggest frugivore, the great curassow; the biggest insectivore, the barred forest-falcon; a specialized predator of social wasp nests, the red-throated caracara; the largest and second largest army-ant followers, the giant ground-cuckoos and the barred woodcreeper (*Dendrocolaptes certhia*); and the largest litter insectivore, the black-faced ant-

The scarlet macaw is dependent on extensive tracts of forest for feeding and nesting. As forests have become fragmented, it has disappeared from much of its former range, particularly in Central America.

thrush. But Barro Colorado Island is still forested, and species reintroductions are therefore possible. For the tiny Palenque forest, however, that option is unavailable. All Palenque gives us is a retrospective, a preliminary measure of what was and is now forever lost.

Were there keel-billed motmots down along the Peñas Blancas gorge? We may never know. After we returned from the search, we backtracked to a vantage point from which we could peer down into the gorge. Someone had followed the river up and performed the usual base alchemy of the tropics: the forest was no more. Instead, pasture and bean fields grew where, perhaps, keel-billed motmots had once flown.

The essence of snake
The foraging tactics of serpents

La Selva Biological Station in the Atlantic lowlands of Costa Rica is now a busy, modern facility replete with telephones, Internet, air-conditioned laboratories, good road access, and a tie to the country's main electrical grid. When I first traveled there over twenty-five years ago, it was still a quiet spot, accessible only by a pleasant boat trip. The supply of electricity was limited to a few hours of thumping diesel generation each evening. On my first night, my only company was Chico, the cook, and after we had demolished a pile of his French fries, he went to bed. I was half asleep myself as I strolled down the path to shut off the generator, my feet clad in cheap thong sandals. I halted in mid-step just as a mottled brown missile tipped with a gaping mouth launched itself at my toes. The force of the pit viper's strike dragged it along the path. But my foot had already recoiled out of range. My body had instinctively reacted to the snake before my brain had formulated a response.

Before the explorer Fawcett disappeared in Amazonia, he wrote of a far more dramatic encounter with a 10-foot-long (3 m) bushmaster. As he was walking along a trail in the lowlands of Bolivia, "all of a sudden, something made me jump sideways and open my legs wide, and between them shot the wicked head and huge body of a striking bushmaster . . . . What amazed me more than anything was the warning of my subconscious mind and the instant muscular response."

Most naturalists have experienced the startle reflex that is set off by an unexpected meeting with a snake. Biologists such as Harvard's E. O. Wilson believe that when humans evolved in Afro-Asia, in the midst of a rich venomous-snake fauna, we developed an instinctive fright response that was triggered by the snake's distinctive form. Neural circuits located well below the plane of consciousness read the data, make the calculations, freeze us in our tracks, and make us back away. As Wilson put it, "The brain appears to have kept its old capacities, its channeled quickness. We stay alert and alive in the vanished forests of the world."

Like most naturalists, I usually keep any ancient fear and loathing of serpents well buried. But in tropical rainforests, I find that a concern about venomous snakes can grow into a paranoia that diminishes only with the passage of time. A few days in the forest are necessary before I stop contemplating each bit of undergrowth I have to step through. It is the dark, three-dimensional character of the rainforest habitat that seems psychologically important; venomous snakes are more abundant in dry scrub and desert habitat, but one worries about them less because of the openness, light, and generally good visibility. What you can contemplate at a distance does not bother you. But, like other rainforest organisms, tropical snakes have radiated into all levels of the forest: many of them are superb tree climbers, others work the shrubbery and vines, some lie in wait on the ground or nose through the leaf litter. Because the rainforest is a habitat of dim shade pierced by fragments of blinding sun, you walk with the knowledge that snakes can be right beside you, almost underfoot or overhead, without your seeing them easily. Rainforests seem to set our mental trigger at its most sensitive level.

The sudden sighting of any snake, whether it is venomous or not, sets off our startle response, because the bodies of all snakes are highly stereotypical. Their basic shape does not vary like that of other animal groups such as mammals, fish, and birds. Snakes

A parrot snake (*Leptophis depressirostris*) in defensive threat display with wide-open mouth.

are stripped-down, streamlined predators—their ecological essence is first and foremost a long, expandable stomach with a mouth at one end. Naturalists will find, however, that in the rainforest, snakes have the most varied and specialized diets of any group of vertebrate predators in spite of their similar form. There are species that eat only snails and slugs, others that specialize in scorpions, and still others that subsist on frog eggs. Some feed only on adult frogs and birds, others only on fish or other snakes. To achieve such a degree of diversity, snakes have had to make the most of their mouths.

Biologists find much to admire in what snakes, working with limited tools, have accomplished as predators. They are a morphologically homogeneous group, lacking limbs to capture and handle prey. Try eating fried chicken without your hands, and you will have a greater appreciation of the problem.

Herpetologist Harry Greene has worked out much of the evolutionary ecology of feeding by snakes. He points out that ancestral snakes were probably lizardlike and used a powerful bite to kill prey, as do some large monitor lizards. Burrowing snakes rely on biting assisted by a little constriction to kill their prey, while boas rely far more on constriction and use their bite to grab rather than to kill. I can remember the first time I saw an anaconda draped in powerful loops; it looked big enough and strong enough to eat almost any animal in its habitat. And true to form, anacondas do, in fact, eat caimans and 100-pound (45 kg) mammals such as wild pigs. Leopards fall prey to Indian pythons, and African pythons can swallow impalas.

The larger snakes may nonetheless be overrated as gourmands. A python may weigh well over 330 pounds (150 kg), yet the heaviest prey it can eat weighs less than half of that. The

Many snakes have a specialized diet. Lamar's snail-eater (*Sibon lamari*), left, is one of a number of species that feed solely on snails and slugs.

The cat-eyed snake (*Leptodeira septentrionalis*), right, often hunts around the margins of swamps and ponds for the eggs of red-eyed leaf frogs (*Agalychnis callidryas*) that have been deposited on leaves above the water.

diameter rather than the weight of the intended prey is the limiting factor; a python overcomes that limitation to some extent by stretching the victim as it swallows it. By contrast, a snake such as a pit viper can kill and ingest a food item heavier than itself. (Admittedly, some marine fish can eat prey of even higher multiples of their own weight, but in their buoyant environment, they do not have to support the weight of the prey.)

Snakes began to diversify into 2,500-odd species only when they developed flexible, specialized mouths. As their bones became smaller and evolved so that they could shift relative to one another, modern snakes acquired the ability to open their mouths a full 150 degrees. A wide gape enables a species like the African egg-eating snake to swallow bird eggs that are three times as wide as its head. The tips of several of the snake's vertebrae project into the gullet and pierce the egg, allowing the snake to squeeze the contents onward and then to expel the nutritionally worthless eggshell. These specialist snakes do all their eating during the bird-breeding season, then fast for the remainder of the year. Humans have been so impressed with the feats of egg-eating snakes that the ancient Egyptians, Cambodians, Hopi, and Maya used snake images to explain lunar and solar eclipses as well as the onset of night and the winter solstice.

It would be misleading, however, to claim that snakes have diverse diets simply because they have wide mouths. The con-

strictor has special muscles that pull the windpipe opening in the floor of its mouth forward and past the prey as it is being swallowed. Its time-consuming, tight-squeeze feeding strategy means that a constrictor could suffocate long before the end of its meal if it were not for those changes in its throat and mouth. The act of swallowing may be assisted by muscles that rotate the jaw forward, then pull it backward, thereby "walking" the head of the snake over the victim. The flexible, erectile fangs typical of the pit viper can also assist in ratcheting the prey down the gullet, an especially useful feature with frogs and toads that swell like balloons when threatened. Snail-eating snakes can rotate their jaws, hook onto the snail and pull it from its shell. Thus the snake is saved the difficulty of swallowing and digesting the shell.

Diet diversity is enhanced by the snake's ability to forage in areas that are difficult to reach. Snakes use their serpentine form to probe rodent runways and ant nests and to twine their way like vines through the treetops. One of the most elegant accessibility adaptations is used by the blunt-headed tree snake (*Imantodes cenchoa*) of Central and South America, which specialize in dining on sleeping anole lizards. Slumbering lizards might seem like easy pickings, but the forest anoles behave in a way that thwarts most predators. They bed down far out on the ends of fern fronds, leaves, and vine tips. The perch vibrates whenever an animal starts

The bright-ringed snake (*Erythrolamprus bizonus*), a coral-snake mimic, is a specialist predator of other snakes. This one is swallowing a cat-eyed snake (*Leptodeira septentrionalis*) tail first.

crawling along the vegetation, and the alerted lizard drops off and runs away. A blunt-headed tree snake is able to circumvent the anole's early-warning system by exploiting its unique anatomy. This snake has a curious triangular, rather than the usual tubular, cross-sectional shape. Its skeletal system is shaped something like an I-beam, and its interlocking vertebrae and vertebral scales prevent the snake from sagging, enabling it to extend fully half of its body out into space without support. The blunt-headed tree snake also has huge, bulging eyes that perhaps help it to spot a lizard at some distance. In any case, the snake crawls along a plant adjacent to a sleeping lizard, reaches through the air without touching the perch, and grasps its unsuspecting prey.

Other snakes draw their prey to them with caudal lures. Some pit vipers sit cryptically coiled, waggling their tail tip seductively, perhaps to attract insectivorous lizards or birds. Prey luring may explain the odd golden form of a common Central American pit viper, the eyelash viper (*Bothrops schlegelii*). These sit-and-wait predators are normally mottled in browns and greens, but herpetologists have long known that sometimes a brood will contain individuals which are brilliant yellow-gold instead, a seeming disadvantage. Michael Fogden has discovered one possible purpose for the distinct coloration. When he found one of the gold vipers coiled around a heliconia inflorescence, a flower that hummingbirds regularly visit, he set up his camera and waited. A hummingbird appeared, hovering before the huge golden "flower," which then lashed out at the hummingbird in a typical feeding strike.

Wonderful as such tactics are, people seem most fascinated by the adaptation many snakes have evolved to handle and control kicking, squirming, biting, and flying prey without the aid of limbs. Venom is a key adaptation. A snake's head has a dozen different glands, many of which produce toxic secretions. Some snakes have venom glands that act in conjunction with specialized muscles and grooved or tubular fangs that enable them to inject the venom. The poison we feel so threatened by is first and foremost a feeding adaptation used to subdue dinner. By using venom to immobilize its prey, a snake has to rely less on a strong bite, and its mouth, as a result, may evolve an even more flexible structure.

Some animal venoms are chemically straightforward concoctions, but most of the five hundred to six hundred species of highly venomous snakes synthesize a remarkably diverse soup. Scientists used to believe that venoms acted as either neurotoxins, which paralyze parts of the nervous system, or haemotoxins, which destroy blood and tissue, and that snakes had either one or the other. But, in fact, many other elements can be found in venoms, including amines, sugars, fats, nucleotides, chemical salts, and enzymes that digest tissue, clot blood, spread fluids, destroy blood cells, interrupt the heartbeat, and block nerve impulses. Each snake species has a unique mixture of molecules. Although physiologists have studied venom chemistry, the ecology of snake venom remains an unexplored frontier. What is known, however, suggests that venom is a complex response to the challenges of foraging and digestion.

The fact that venoms are primarily a feeding adaptation also seems reflected in the seasonality of their production. Studies of snakes like the Persian and African carpet vipers show that venom production peaks in summer and declines sharply in autumn and winter—paralleling the snake's natural cycle of feeding and fasting. Similarly, most venomous snakes avoid wasting venom on a nonfood item. Given the opportunity to escape, most do not bite, and even those which strike defensively often do not deliver much venom. Altruism is not involved; venom is a necessity for feeding and is time-consuming to manufacture. For example, when a rattlesnake is milked, more than a month is required for it to replenish its venom supply completely, although it will have produced enough in three days to be dangerous again.

Consider the venom of the fer-de-lance, the most dangerous snake in Central America; this species accounts for more than half of the thousands of snakebites that occur each year and for most of the fatalities. The fer-de-lance is known for both the tremendous quantity and the potency of its venom, as well as its pugnacious disposition. A large adult fer-de-lance can produce close to 0.43 cubic inches (7 cm³) of liquid venom with a dry weight of some 0.05 ounces (1.5 g), which makes it the greatest venom producer of all pit vipers. A lethal intravenous dose for adult humans is estimated at only 0.001 to 0.004 ounces (40 to 110 mg). Although at first it might seem to be unnecessarily powerful, this particularly toxic and abundant brew appears to be profoundly suited to the task confronting the hungry fer-de-lance.

The hog-nosed viper (*Porthidium nasutum*) feeds on small vertebrates, including whip-tailed lizards (*Ameiva festiva*), top, and rain frogs (*Eleutherodactylus* sp.), bottom. Vipers have a flexible jaw apparatus, allowing them to swallow prey items greater than their own body weight.

As an adult, the heavy-bodied snake coils on the ground, often near game trails, and waits for opossums, rodents, and other mammals to pass within striking range. Then it opens its jaws, erects its fangs, and smacks the animal. The fangs act like hypodermics about 1 inch (2 to 3 cm) long, squirting venom deep into the victim. Small species of pit vipers or juvenile fer-de-lances hang on to their prey, but the adult fer-de-lance never grips its prey. It withdraws immediately after striking and waits for the venom to work. The victim may wander about a little but soon is immobilized. (The smaller tree-dwelling pit viper, by contrast, clings to its prey and does not let it drop.) After a few minutes, the fer-de-lance uncoils and follows the mammal's trail by collecting the plume of scent in the air with its flickering tongue and reading it with a special Jacobson's organ in its mouth; it can also detect body warmth with a pair of special sensors located in its face. The pit viper owes its popular name to the pitlike infrared detecting organs whose diaphragms are capable of registering temperature differences as slight as two-tenths of a degree.

Predators such as the fer-de-lance economize on energy by not actively searching for prey, but in turn, they must fully exploit their rather uncommon encounters with prey. A typical meal consists of a single large item rather than many smaller ones. Pit vipers like the fer-de-lance represent the maximum development of this tendency, eating heavier prey for their size than do large, nonvenomous snakes. This capacity allows them to swallow prey that weighs 150 percent of their own weight.

Like most snakes, the fer-de-lance has loose jaw articulations and thin, flexible ribs that expand outward as a large body is swallowed. The advantages of this expansive ability are considerable. Herpetologist Carl Gans calculates that a small increase in the diameter of the swallowed object makes for a relatively large increase in volume. A 10 percent increase in diameter, for example, means 21 percent more volume to be ingested. But the snake's accommodating architecture makes the absolute immobility of its prey necessary. The flexibility of snake ribs makes them delicate, and a twitching, kicking mammal might easily damage them. There is, in fact, a record of a boa constrictor—a snake that does not envenomate its prey—being killed by an anteater that the boa had partially swallowed.

Fer-de-lance venom not only kills its prey rapidly but also speeds up the digestive process, a particularly important adaptation for a cold-blooded organism that does not chew its food. A mammal is packaged in a tough, furry hide; by injecting its prey, the snake starts the digestive process from the inside out. Various enzymes in the venom begin to break down blood and tissue, and other enzymes spread the mixture rapidly through the body. When the fer-de-lance is deprived of its venom glands, feeding takes three to four times as long—twelve days to digest a rat, for instance, instead of the usual three or four days.

The large pit vipers are known for the haemorrhagic impact of their venom even when it is diluted in the much larger human body. I heard a firsthand account of a plantation worker in Ecuador who stepped squarely on a bushmaster that delivered a full and fatal injection of venom. The victim reportedly began to bleed through every mucous membrane as the venom rapidly at-

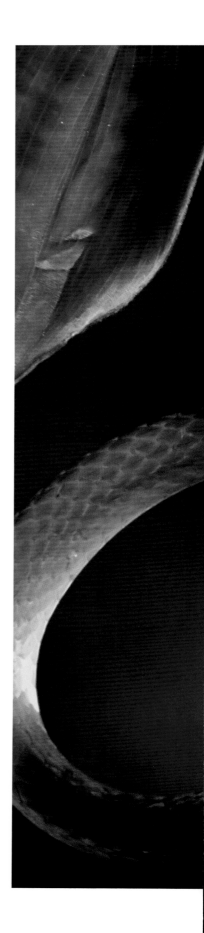

The green vine snake (*Oxybelis fulgidus*) possesses an extremely thin, elongate green body, a combination that provides excellent camouflage as it hunts through tangled vegetation in search of anole lizards.

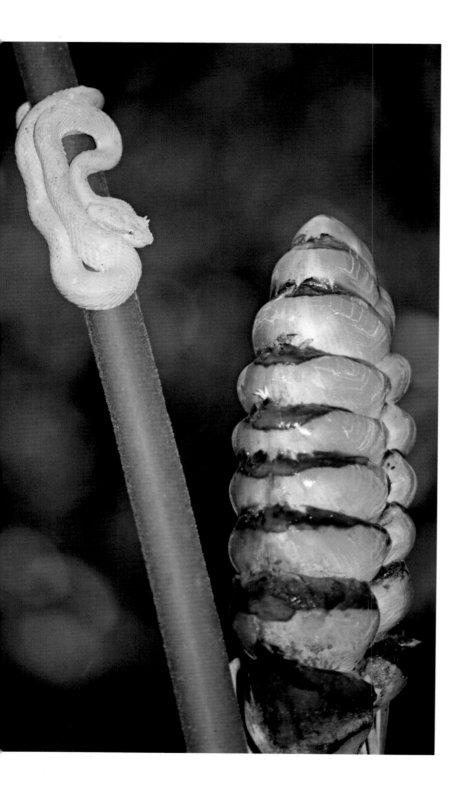

A golden eyelash viper (*Bothriechis schlegelii*) lies in wait to ambush hummingbirds attracted to the large, colorful flower bracts of *Heliconia imbricata*.

tacked the circulatory system. Students of Brazilian *Bothrops* bites relate that "when the venom quantity injected by the bite is high, one may observe haemorrhages from the mucous membranes of the nose and gums, from the margins of the fingernails, from the skin of the head, even from the stomach." Imagine the effect of this on an opossum.

This ecological view of snake venom leads me to wonder if it is mere coincidence that the venom of a high-altitude pit viper living in the cool, misty forest on a Central American mountain has the greatest ability to cause haemorrhagic destruction of tissue. Lowland species of pit vipers and rattlesnakes have much lower haemorrhagic impacts. Perhaps that reflects the greater need of the cool-climate pit vipers to increase their digestive rate through a venom designed to enhance the enzymatic breakdown of tissues. The lowland species can rely instead on the heat of the tropical sun and air and on conventional digestive enzymes to speed digestion along.

The paralytic toxicity of venoms also varies according to feeding ecology. Sea snakes, for example, have a radically different venom from that of the fer-de-lance. Hunting live fish in a three-dimensional environment increases the chance that the prey will be able to escape. In addition, fish are more easily digested than are mammals. Digestive breakdown is thus less important to a sea snake than is the rapid immobilization of the fish. Accordingly, when a sea snake strikes a fish, it delivers only a small amount of venom with little digestive impact. But the tremendously potent venom paralyzes the fish in seconds; a gram of some types of sea-snake venom would be enough to kill a thousand people, a potency some fifty to a hundred times greater than that of fer-de-lance venom.

No matter how potent the weaponry, there is usually an organism that has evolved a counteradaptation. A high degree of resistance to rattlesnake venom is found in the common Virginia opossum, which can endure a dose sixty times greater than the amount normally lethal to other mammals. An injection strong enough to kill a horse produces only a slight change in heartbeat in the opossum, and within half an hour, the animal shows no effect whatsoever. That adaptation enables the opossum to treat a swamp infested with rattlers and the related water moccasins and copperheads not as a health hazard but as a feeding opportunity. Interestingly, the opossum shows no resistance to cobra venom. That makes good evolutionary sense, since the Virginia opossum is naturally distributed in areas where rattlesnakes abound but cobras do not. Domestic cats, on the other hand, which evolved in the cobra-rich regions of Egypt, the Middle East, and India, remain rather resistant to cobra venom. Similarly, mongooses are eight times more resistant to cobra venom than are rabbits, animals that have not coevolved with cobras.

Habitual snake-eating raptors such as white hawks and laughing falcons probably rely more on their heavily scaled legs than on an immunity to the poison to survive a venomous attack. To protect itself further, a laughing falcon, upon landing on a snake, will immediately bite off its prey's head. Nevertheless, there is a record of a red-tailed hawk dying with a coral snake in its talons, exhibiting the typical symptoms of paralysis and evidence of hav-

ing been bitten in the leg. That may explain why birds such as motmots, which feed on snakes and whose range closely overlaps that of coral snakes, reportedly avoid coral snakes instinctively, and why so many snakes have a banding pattern similar to the coral snake's.

Snake-eating snakes such as king cobras, king snakes, and indigo snakes are thought to be immune to many kinds of snake venom. That natural immunity is what allows snakes like the mussurana to specialize in a diet of other snakes, including the highly toxic fer-de-lance. Such a specialization makes the mussurana (*Clelia clelia*) one of the few snakes to be cherished by *campesinos* throughout Latin America.

As a rule, of course, snakes are not generally appreciated; people the world over wage war on them every chance they get,

The golden eyelash viper is able to hunt at night, as well as by day, using the large loreal pits located in front of its eyes. These organs are sensitive to infrared radiation and are effective in targeting small, warm-blooded animals.

despite the fact that, statistically, they have little to fear. But a heightened alertness and instinctive wariness occasioned by the knowledge that there are venomous snakes about will always remain part of the rainforest milieu. We can temper our ancient adaptive aversion with respect and with cautious admiration for a group of predators that has managed to make so much of such minimal equipment.

Monteverde
Higher & drier

La Cascada in the Monteverde Cloud Forest Preserve—an area important for the survival of many rare and endangered species. The preserve lies within a region of endemism comprising the highlands of Costa Rica and western Panama. Isolated for millions of years, these highlands are home to numerous plants and animals that occur nowhere else in the world. Many of the endemics are, or in some cases were, found in the preserve, including nearly 30 different bird species, 13 reptiles, and 24 amphibians.

The Monteverde Cloud Forest Preserve is being badly affected by the world's changing climate. Global warming has raised the average height at which clouds form and the cloud forest is now immersed in mist less frequently than it used to be. The beautiful sight of sunbeams piercing drifting mist, left, is becoming rarer. The reduction in mist is important because the cloud forest typically derives up to half its total moisture from wind-driven clouds passing through the trees. With less mist there is less moisture to support the lush and varied growth of plants, top right, and moss, bottom right, that is so characteristic of the cloud forest.

Because of global warming, many species characteristic of the Monteverde cloud forest are retreating uphill. For example, the collared redstart, left, and the resplendent quetzal, right, no longer breed in many of the lower areas that they occupied in the 1980s and 1990s.

More than thirty years ago, for reasons that now seem dim and curious, I found myself in Guanacaste, Costa Rica, studying the social life of tropical hornets. Guanacaste was sun-baked and windblown throughout its long dry season. But it did have an abundance and diversity of large hornet nests. Usually this was a good thing. But occasionally the attractions of this pursuit wore thin, especially after an attempt to catch and mark a large colony of wasps had gone painfully wrong. Some nights, as I lay alone in my dusty bed, sweating, with some body part throbbing from wasp venom, while the fierce trade winds shook the roof and rattled the shutters, I dreamed of the cloud forests around Monteverde.

Half a day's drive away up the mountain slopes was a lush virid paradise. To be sure there was plenty of wind in Monteverde, but it was cool and laden with mist. It was a pleasure to be up there, sitting in the mossy lee of an epiphyte-laden tree, watching the scudding clouds coming from the Caribbean side and sailing across the Continental Divide. As the clouds crossed to the Pacific slope they often thinned into drifting mist. On the wispy leading edge of these mists, the water droplets acted as a trillion tiny prisms, and then the drifting rainbow they made would dissolve as the droplets sifted down onto the vegetation.

The mist made it a good place for those of an amphibian persuasion. Walking at night I would routinely see tree frogs and sala-

manders lollygagging on the leaves, their skin moist and glistening in the light of my headlamp. Of course, it was an amphibian that put Monteverde on the map for biologists. The once amazing golden toad, the males of which were a hallucinatory intense golden orange, was found only there. This toad was first reported by Jerry James, one of the Quaker dairy farmers who settled Monteverde and who eventually created the Monteverde Cloud Forest Preserve to protect the breeding habitat of the golden toad. The male toads would congregate by the hundreds around the temporary pools made by the first heavy spring rains. They waited for females to arrive and stimulate the copulatory frenzy that preceded egg laying in these pools. The golden toad was last seen in 1989.

Monteverde had many such biological enchantments. I remember sitting at the base of an *Ocotea* tree looking down the slope of a green pastured hill. The tree, a cousin of the avocado, was laden with small, brilliant green fruits the size of olives, each held aloft in display by a brilliant red stem. The spectacle attracted resplendent quetzals. A couple of males and a female perched toward the base of the slope in a fig, and made forays, flapping upslope to collect a fruit and then returning to their perch to swallow it. Approaching the *Ocotea*, the quetzals were nearly level with my face when they tilted back to hover briefly and acrobatically twist to pluck their quarry. The morning light lit up the brilliant, flailing iridescence of serpentine tail feathers as long as my arm. I could see why the Mixtec, Olmecs, Aztecs, and later the Mayans incorporated these iconic birds into the deity Quetzalcoatl, the feathered serpent—an inventive god that variously created maize farming, calendars, and books.

The presence of quetzals right within sight of human habitation was one of the pleasures to be had amid the patchwork of dairy farms that made up the Monteverde community. The quetzals were commonly seen foraging in the isolated fruiting trees left standing in pastures, and they made their nests in the soft moldering wood of dead snags. Now global warming pushes them higher up the mountain slope.

We know this because of the assiduous observations by long-term Monteverde resident and biologist Alan Pounds, who began studying cloud-forest reptiles and amphibians in the early 1980s. At the same time, Michael Fogden also began observing reptiles, amphibians, and birds in the Monteverde area. Weather data was simultaneously collected by the late John Cambell, a dairy farmer who lived in Monteverde. Taken together these observations paint a disturbing picture. We know now the dry season runs longer, the clouds form higher on the mountain, and the driving mist attenuates earlier. This local climate change is driven by factors that may include the increase of sea temperature, the loss of lowland forest, and perhaps an elevation of air temperatures. Its biological effects are now broadly manifest.

Birds that were common lower down, such as keel-billed toucans, now commingle with the quetzals. The quetzals, who become carnivorous when rearing young, used to catch cloud-forest anole lizards and frogs. These prey species have retreated up the mountain and have been replaced by species more characteristic of the drier, hotter lower slopes.

Michael Fogden recently wrote me the following appraisal of what has transpired in Monteverde's herpetological community:

Snakes crashed at about the same time as frogs. In a total of 17 months from 1986 to 1987, I noted exactly 100 colubrid snakes of 22 species in the Monteverde/Peñas Blancas area. By contrast, in 19 months from 1994 to 1997, I encountered only 12 colubrids snakes of only 8 species. The situation is even worse if the Monteverde area is considered alone. I used to see at least 5 to 6 snakes every month, but in 26 months spread over the past seven years (2000 to 2006) I have seen only 6 snakes in total!

The anole situation is equally dire. It used to be possible to find 50+ sleeping *Norops tropidolepis* in 2-3 hours around our house. Now there are none, though we can usually find one or two if we search as far as La Cascada on the Río Trail. *Norops altae* used to be common, but none have been seen anywhere in the preserve for years. We see a few *Norops intermedius* and *woodi*, and a few *humilis* have moved upslope. But the total numbers now are tiny. I could not guarantee to find even a single anole of any species in a night of searching on our land.

Possibly the decline of snakes (most of which eat frogs) is related to the decline of frogs, but I doubt it is the whole story. In any case, anoles have crashed just as dramatically and they don't eat frogs.

For some species, such as the golden toad, the retreat has been absolute and for others extreme. In the 1980s, Alan Pounds took me to one of his study sites in the upper reaches of the Largarto River. The vegetation was already heavily degraded, save a strip along the margins of the boulder-strewn stream. Every couple of yards one could spot harlequin toads, a species almost as spectacular as the golden toad. Harlequin toads had toxic skin, which presumably explains why they could sit conspicuously exposed on rocks in broad daylight. But they were not without natural enemies. They were eaten by an unusual species of flesh fly. Most members of this family feed on carrion; but this particular fly species laid its maggots on the frog, and its larvae burrowed in and ate the frog from the inside out—"a fly that eats frogs," as Pounds called it. However, it was a fungus, not a fly, that actually did this toad in. Most of the amphibians seem to have died from fungal skin infections. Pounds believes that climate change made conditions favorable for fungal epidemics to attack montane frogs.

An insoluble conundrum confronts the Monteverde plants and animals that depend on cool and humid conditions. The mountains in central Costa Rica are low, so there is no nearby place for these species to climb to refind their climate. And for species that depend on predictable rains, such as the golden toad, even greater elevational relief may not have made a difference.

In the 1980s, when I spent my winters in Monteverde, we biologists and a good number of the farmers used to worry a lot about deforestation. We created a successful conservation NGO (the Monteverde Conservation League), we wrote articles and grant proposals, gave talks to raise money, and then we bought forest and expanded the protected area. We worked with farmers to reforest windbreaks. As a result, plenty of cloud forest remains in the Monteverde area. I have no doubt that the labors of the many people to conserve habitat have made the ecological health of Monteverde's forests immeasureably better than it would have been otherwise. Yet protecting habitat was not enough. The skies and the clouds were beyond our reach.

In the past twenty years, the lower boundary of the Monteverde cloud forest has been invaded by a dozen or more bird species that were formerly found only in lower, drier areas, including chestnut-headed oropendolas, left, and keel-billed toucans, right.

The extinction of the golden toad (*Bufo periglenes*), top left, one of the flagship species of Monteverde, attracted a lot of publicity. It disappeared with startling rapidity. It was present in normal numbers in 1987, but only one adult (a male) was found at breeding pools in 1988 and 1989. Many other amphibians (salamanders as well as frogs) disappeared at the same time. A few have recolonized the area but most of the higher elevation species are still missing and as many as seven or eight may be extinct. Among the latter is the Monteverde harlequin frog (*Atelopus* sp.), bottom left, which disappeared even before it had been given a scientific name.

It is not just diversity that has declined. The surviving species are present in very low numbers, generally less than 10 percent of their former abundance. There used to be three hundred territorial Fleischmann's glass frogs (*Hyalinobatrachium fleischmanni*), top right, along a short stretch of the Guacimal River. Now there are never more than a handful. And golden-eyed leaf frogs (*Agalychnis annae*), bottom right, are hardly ever seen. There is abundant evidence that a chytrid fungus (*Batrachochytrium dendrobatidis*) is implicated in the declines and extinctions of the golden toad, harlequin frogs, and other amphibians. Declines correlate with the warmest years, however, suggesting that climate change is the root of the problem.

The disappearance of amphibians from the Monteverde Cloud Forest Preserve has been widely publicized. It is not so well known that snakes and anoles have declined just as dramatically. Populations of both crashed in the Monteverde area at about the same time as amphibians. Among the species that have been most severely affected are the cloud forest anole (*Norops tropidolepis*), top left; montane anole (*Norops altae*), bottom left; green racer (*Chironius exoletus*), above; and fire-bellied snake (*Liophis epinephalus*), right.

The profusion of epiphytes that grow on cloud forest trees is obviously vulnerable to reduced misting and long runs of dry days. Orchids, particularly miniature species, such as *Sigmatostalix guatemalensis*, top left, *Dichaea muricata*, bottom left, and *Platystele* sp., right, are exceptionally diverse in the cloud forest and many already appear to be less abundant than they used to be. Epiphytes play a crucial role in the cloud forest. They have the ability to assimilate airborne nutrients that would otherwise be lost, and they interact with many other species by providing shelter and food. Any significant reduction of epiphytes is likely to have consequences that reverberate throughout the system.

Fruits of reason
Interpreting the meaning of tropical fruit

Finding a rainforest fruit is a bit like finding an ancient, tattered historical manuscript. Parts of it may be missing or obscure, but it will contain characteristics that we can read and interpret. Fruits eaten by bats, for example, are typically dull-colored or white. We do not expect them to be otherwise, because the only animals in the forest with good color vision are birds and monkeys, and fruits that signal ripening with bright colors are probably catering to them.

Placement and presentation are also important. If a fruit dangles from the tips of branches, we suspect that a flying or highly acrobatic animal is involved. When large seeds come packaged in tough protective layers, gnawing, scatter-hoarding rodents and perhaps strong-jawed peccaries are implicated. With the exception of some vultures and a few seabirds, a bird's sense of smell is not acute, so if a fruit's ripening is announced with a strong odor, we suspect it might be a food source for mammals; we can also look for correlated factors such as size to discern just what mammalian species might be attracted.

The most highly scented fruit is the durian, which grows in the rainforests of Southeast Asia. Weighing several pounds, it is so fearsomely spiked that without its stalk, it is painful to carry. No bird or arboreal animal appears strong enough to breach its foul-smelling armor to get at the white pulp and chestnut-sized seeds inside. When ripe, the durian is renowned for both its reek and its taste.

The boldly patterned bill of the chestnut-mandibled toucan is used in social communication, but its primary function is to reach for food, in this case the fruits of a nutmeg tree (*Virola koschnyi*).

Yet Alfred Russel Wallace argued that the chance to eat one was worth a voyage to the East, and the Dyaks of Borneo have been known to camp for days in the forest, waiting for the fruit to fall from the trees. Nevertheless, most people compare the experience of eating durian to that of consuming a sublime custard while sitting next to an open sewer. In the West, hotels often post signs forbidding guests to bring disreputable visitors to their rooms. In the East, hotels unanimously oppose the entry of durians. As Wallace remarked, durians instruct us that fruits "do not appear to be organized with exclusive reference to the use and convenience of man." Instead, the repulsive smell, combined with the size of the fruit and seed and the fact that the spiky fruit remains unripe until it falls to the ground, suggests that the durian caters to such stalwart terrestrial mammals as rhinoceroses, elephants, and pigs. Indeed, Asian elephants reportedly use their trunks to roll fallen durians in mud, thus clogging and coating the spines; then they bolt them down whole.

Such detective work sounds simple. But the only simple truth about fruits is that they all "want" to be eaten. They have, indeed, evolved characteristics that attract dispersal agents. But which ones? Many fruits serve more than one master. Rare is the fruit that is not eaten by a panoply of species, each of which has a different impact on the plant. *Muntingia* trees, which grow along rivers in Central and South America, have cherry-sized fruits that are red and sweet; one might suppose that birds are their dispersers, yet bats also feed heavily on them.

One learns about fruits with the eyes, fingers, and nose. The tongue is also important, although you soon learn to use it with some caution. Sweetly benign fruits are rare in the rainforest, the result of the complex ecological pressures that affect a fruit's evolution. The evolutionary interest of plants is clearly uppermost, so

they may evolve properties not entirely to the benefit of some frugivores. It is conceivable—and some of my experience suggests—that many fruits are designed to promote rapid gut passage of the seeds, a trait with messy maladaptive consequences when introduced into the human digestive system (and social system, for that matter) but one that may not bother kinkajous and spider monkeys.

It is a sad fact that the great variety of rainforest fruits does not translate into an abundance of food for the hungry naturalist. I can perhaps find more good fruits to eat in a temperate zone than I can in a tropical rainforest. Those who have enjoyed papaya, pineapple, mango, and other domesticated fruits of the tropics are often surprised to find that of the thousands of varieties of rainforest fruits, only a few are fit for human consumption when taken as is from the wild. They do exist, but it is difficult to tell which of the dozens of fruits you might find on a morning walk in the rainforest are edible.

I have, however, recently found a wild tropical fruit I enjoy eating. It grows in clusters at the ends of the branches of a *Saurauia* treelet, a relative of the kiwi fruit that is found in edges and light gaps in montane rainforest and cloud forest in Costa Rica. *Saurauia* fruit is not attractive, either to look at or to eat. It is a drab greenish-brown, slightly flattened sphere the size of a quarter, and is protected by strong bracts at the base. The skin is tough, slightly hairy, and inedible. The locals call the fruit *moco*, which is Spanish for nasal mucus, and when I bit into one, I found out why.

When you sink your teeth into a *moco* fruit, a slimy substance bursts forth. The liquid's texture is unique—cohesive but not sticky. The clear fluid, which is impregnated with a mass of tiny black seeds, often forms a long, ropy strand, resembling a fluid vermicelli noodle, that can be slurped up no matter how far out of your mouth it dangles. In addition to its admirable tactile qualities, the fruit is sweet and has a mild yet distinctive flavor.

What is the *moco* designed for? I suspect that its combination of features implicates bats as the agents of dispersal. The fruit has little color, is tough-skinned and sweet, has a high moisture content, and contains hundreds of hard, tiny seeds suitable for being swallowed and then dispersed over the open and edge habitats where this weedy tree is found. Strengthening my belief is the fact that I have found strong bite marks on the fruit that are characteristic of those made by bats.

For every *moco* in the rainforest, there are a hundred unpleasant or insipid fruits, and it is never easy to assess which fruit is palatable and which might be toxic. The experimenter who samples indiscriminately faces certain hazards. In choosing a fruit, one cannot follow the lead of our closest rainforest relatives, the primates. The figs they eat are often acrid rather than sweet. Others have a nasty, lingering aftertaste. Nor will it help to observe birds. Many birds favor large, greasy fare. They will eat both bland, tasteless berries and tiny tepin chili peppers that are hot enough to cause a burned yellowing of the fingertips when you pick them and excruciating pain if you taste one. *Terminalia* fruits, which are consumed by parrots, may be half tannin, the same astringent compound used to turn skin into leather.

Plants advertise their fruit in massive displays or with contrasting colors to attract birds, a group of dispersers with excellent color vision. The fruits of *Simaruba glauca*, left, become black as they ripen. The red pods of this leguminous tree (*Pithecellobium unguis-cati*), above, split open to reveal a nutritious white aril attached to the black seeds.

The fruits of *Clusia* trees, left, are capsules that split open when ripe, revealing brightly colored arils that attract many frugivorous birds.

A scarlet macaw, right, bites into the tough, outer layer of a fruit of a tropical almond tree (*Terminalia catappa*) to get at the seed. Although often described as fruit-eaters, macaws and parrots are usually after seeds. For the most part, they are seed predators rather than seed dispersers.

The combined task of attraction and defense often produces a fruit that is a mix of reward and punishment. The seed must be defended against large predators like macaws and squirrels or perhaps against the mechanical and biochemical hazards of a disperser's digestive tract. To defend its soft flesh against fungi or bacteria, a fruit may produce antibiotics and oils that we find unpleasant. The thymol that is found in orange skin is an antibiotic essential oil. The valuation of such properties depends on the desperation of the frugivore. Biting into orange peel may be unpleasant, but many birds and mammals, when truly hungry, think nothing of the slightly bitter task of breaching the skin to extract the sugar and vitamins inside. Specialized dispersers reduce the costs of ingesting such defensive compounds by evolving means of overcoming the toxins that defend or restrict access to many fruits. Some Asian bats dine with impunity on *Strychnos* tree fruits, which contain enough strychnine to kill large mammals.

This conflict of interest may be behind the fantastic molecular complexity packaged in a fruit. The rewards may be sugars, fats, proteins, starches, and vitamins in various combinations, presented with attractive pigments, alluring odors that signal ripeness, and hormones that regulate the ripening. Large seeds are often heavily defended by an array of compounds. Coca seeds, for instance, are coated in a soft, white, sweet pulp, but the seed is a mass of chemicals. More than seven hundred compounds are found in the coca powder made from the seeds, and many of these compounds are bitter and defensive in function.

A fruit is designed to maximize the plant's gains while minimizing its costs. Plants are not above duplicity. Some outright mimicry occurs in certain legumes such as *Ormosia*, which imitates the nutritious red and black coating used as advertising by hundreds of species of plants. *Ormosia* has only a hard, inedible coat with no rewards; the seed has to be spit out after the bird has swooped down and plucked it from the exposed seedpod. To swallow it may be fatal, as *Ormosia* and similar legumes are defended with potent alkaloids. The bright, hard seeds are often made into necklaces that are sold to unwitting tourists whose children may chew the seeds, with—in rare instances—fatal results.

Some plants even fake sweetness. The miracle fruit (*Synsepalum dulcificum*), a sapote from Africa, contains a protein that not only mimics the sweet effect of sugar—in fact, it is five thousand times sweeter—but also temporarily prevents the mammalian tongue from detecting bitterness. If one chews the miracle ber-

Along with dozens of other bird species, the golden-hooded tanager, left, is attracted to *Miconia* trees, which produce a large crop of small, sweet fruits with small seeds.

While some monkeys are specialized fruit-eaters, the white-faced monkey, right, is an opportunist feeder, taking fruit, insects, and small vertebrates.

ries and then tastes a sweet orange and a sour lemon, both seem equally sweet. Perhaps the compound is employed by the miracle fruit to mask the bitterness of its own defensive secondary compounds. It is also possible that producing a small amount of protein sweetener is far more economical than manufacturing the large quantity of sugar that other plants use to equal its effect.

All these conflicts of interest and the chemical and ecological complications do not completely thwart us, however. The human brain, addicted as it is to pattern recognition, begins to identify groups of characteristics. For the fleshy fruits, one convenient breakdown is big and small seeds—a quality versus quantity dichotomy.

The many members of the small-seed syndrome include a diversity of shrubs in the coffee, nightshade, blueberry, and melastome families that have small red, orange, or blue-black fruits. In this syndrome, we can also place such fruits as the clustered masses of orange nettle berries, the upright white spikes of pipers, the dangling spikes of *Cecropia*, and many figs. All have numerous tiny seeds that are swallowed whole and passed intact through the digestive system. These seeds are marked by an absence of heavy defensive compounds. Most are too small to bother with,

and only parrots and pigeons have evolved specialized features to grind some of them down. The fruits are often sweet and watery and enjoy a wide and unspecialized patronage. One study of *Cecropia* in Suriname recorded eight species of monkeys, twelve bat species, and seventy-six species of birds eating its fruit.

There is a logical connection between sweetness and the scattergun approach of such plants. The production of sugar requires sunlight, and this dispersal system includes many pioneer plants that colonize open areas such as landslides, tree falls, and riverbanks. *Conostegia* and *Miconia*, for example, are common melastomes in the rainforests of Costa Rica. Their seeds are often packaged in accessible, abundant, and sweet berries produced in crops of tens of thousands per tree. They are eaten by dozens of bird species. The result is a seed blanket that covers the ground. All that is required is the opportunity to sprout into sunlight, and uniform legions of *Conostegia* begin to appear. When a pasture is created out of forest and then allowed to regrow, a monoculture of *Conostegia* shoots up so synchronously and evenly that, within a few years, the area looks like a plantation.

Almost every fruit-eating bird eats *Conostegia*, but no bird depends on it. Small-seeded fruits often do not possess an abun-

Specialized fruit-eaters such as the resplendent quetzal, above, have a relatively wide gape that enables them to swallow wild avocados (*Ocotea* spp.) and then regurgitate the seeds intact and ready to germinate.

dance of fats or oils, and birds and other animals that invariably feed on them must include much insect protein in their diet. Many use a mix of small fruits as a casual source of carbohydrates; neither fruit nor frugivore seems tightly bound species to species. Instead, the syndrome is shaped by vastly diffuse interactions that occur in the temperate zones as well as in the tropics.

By contrast, large, heavy-seeded, nutritious tropical fruits depend on a narrower range of truly specialized dispersal agents. This group includes many primary-forest trees, which often produce a large seed with a highly nutritious coating. An avocado is this theme taken to an extreme. The impact of these fruits is reflected in the unique birds one sees in tropical forests. The most specialized fruit-eating birds, such as toucans, are designed to eat large fruit. Toucans are a truly tropical bird; some forty species are confined to the New World. They have ecological counterparts in the hornbills of Asian and African forests, but no temperate bird is remotely similar.

My favorite species of toucan is the keel-billed, a large bird that sports an appendage almost as long as its body. Its bill is red-tipped with a blend of yellow and green above and blue below, highlighted by a central flare of orange. It looks like the work of an uninhibited watercolorist determined to use all the complementary strength and diversity of the color spectrum. The hue no doubt plays a role in the toucan's social semaphore of bill waving and clashing and its concert of stances that feature its brilliant yellow chest and scarlet rump patch. Yet bills are primarily food-processing devices, and the toucan's is no exception. The toucan uses its long bill to hunt lizards and to pluck bird nestlings out of the depths of tree holes or from the hanging baskets of oropendola nests. It is even known to snap its massive bill at the prospect of minuscule termites in flight. But as Henry Bates suggested, the toucan's bill is first and foremost a fruit-plucking organ.

Most frugivores are catholic in their choices, but the toucan is prodigiously so, and its lengthy bill allows it to exploit a wide range of fruits. The great ornithologist Alexander Skutch made many observations that document this; indeed, anyone who watches a toucan in a fruiting tree will see that the bill enables it to eat fruits denied birds with lesser equipment. The toucan is a relatively heavy bird that feeds while perched on limbs. Whereas many monkeys use their long arms and prehensile tails to reach the outer crown, where fruits often grow, the toucan employs the long forceps provided by its bill. It reaches down, up, ahead, and behind to pluck fruit. Because of its long bill, a toucan has to throw its head back to toss the fruit into its gullet. The bird can also reverse the process, and it is fine entertainment to watch large fruits seemingly vanish and then suddenly materialize again in the toucan's bill.

Quetzals and other fruit-loving trogons feed in a completely different and more limited manner. They flutter up and hover briefly as they pluck the fruit. Instead of investing in a long bill, trogons have evolved huge chest muscles that enable them to pause in midair to make their selection. Nevertheless, it is the toucans that achieve the greatest breadth of diet. In Monteverde, Costa Rica, emerald toucanets feed on some eighty-three species, while resplendent quetzals take only forty-three species.

Fruit is so abundant in the rainforest that specialist frugivores, like this male Andean cock-of-the-rock, are free to spend much of their time calling and displaying on perches to attract the attention of females.

Toucans and quetzals are both highly specialized frugivores that feed on relatively large fruits. But of the two, resplendent quetzals are especially dependent on a particular family of trees, the laurels, or wild avocados (*Lauraceae*). Nat Wheelwright, an ecologist who studied quetzals in Monteverde, found that they fed on all eighteen species of the family that occurred in the area and that these trees accounted for 80 percent of the seeds recovered from seed traps placed near quetzal nests. Quetzals reputedly can breed only where wild avocados occur. That is not because wild avocados provide the sole food for nestlings or adults; the parents also carry in insects such as leaf-eating scarab beetles and even anole lizards to meet the high demands of early nestling growth. But later the nestlings are fed lauraceous fruits, which are extremely rich in oil and protein.

The avocado tree of commerce, which is just a small modification of the native tree, produces a fruit that has as much as 34 percent oil and 20 percent protein. That represents an astounding nutritional investment in a fruit and appears to be a unique evolutionary concession to the biology of specialized frugivorous birds in exchange for dispersal of massive seeds.

The bird that makes the most of this oily reward seems to be the famous oilbird, which lives in caves and echolocates and forages at night, eating only the fruits that it feeds its nestlings. The young bird grows slowly, requiring about one hundred and ten days to fledge, a rate allowable by virtue of its protected nest site on an inaccessible subterranean ledge. Stuffed for weeks with greasy, regurgitated pulp, the nestling ends up like a seal pup, dwarfing its providers. At a little over a pound (six hundred grams), it outweighs an adult bird by 50 percent because of its store of fat. So great is the oil content of the nestlings that when Humboldt first heard about oilbird caves, they were referred to as "mines of fat." Missionaries collected the nestlings for their oil. Ironically, the oilbirds, for all their dependence on fruit, probably kill as many seeds as they disperse. David Snow, author of *The Web of Adaptation*, spent four and a half years collecting seeds in an oilbird cave in Trinidad. He found that "the floor of the cave is deep with an accumulation of decayed and decaying seeds, supporting a seething mass of cockroaches and other insects and crowned with a small forest of etiolated seedlings which spring up readily in the rich compost but soon wither in the absence of light." For the trees, however, the oilbirds represent just one element in a vast amount of seed wastage. Suitable oilbird caves are rare, and oilbird colonies constitute only a minor selective pressure.

In the case of the more widely distributed and once abundant quetzals, the interaction between bird and fruit has yielded more symmetrical dependencies and outcomes. Like the toucan, the quetzal shows morphological adaptations that enable it to swallow lauraceous fruits whole. It is astounding to watch a quetzal accomplish this vanishing act. The bird flies up to a limb, briefly hovers, then yanks a fruit away and returns to a convenient perch with the fruit still held in its mouth. Often blue-black and elongate, the fruit is the size of a large Greek olive, and it looks as big as the quetzal's head. The bird turns it lengthwise in its bill, and then the fruit disappears. Like most specialized frugivores, the quetzal has a huge gape relative to its body size, which matches the size of the fruits the various *Lauraceae* produce, and a digestive system that handles the fruit softly. Instead of the powerful crushing gizzard that seed predators like turkeys have, quetzals, toucans, and the like have an expansive esophagus and a flexible gizzard that removes the fruit pulp but does not harm the seed, which is regurgitated intact and capable of germination. This reduces gut-passage times for both bird and seed and means that the bird does not have to fly about carrying a weighty ballast. These seeds present a marked contrast to those eaten by spider monkeys. Monkeys usually swallow fruit seeds whole rather than chewing them, and certain specialized fruits such as the orange *Diospyros, Manilkara, Brosimum, Pouteria*, and some sapotes have hard seed coats designed to weather the gut passage. Birds tend to regurgitate seeds that are impregnated with digestion-inhibiting toxic alkaloids.

Quetzals and wild avocados have further coevolved in the sense that each makes the life history of the other ecologically possible. Even the most specialized frugivores destroy many seeds by dropping them near the parent tree. There is a whole guild of animals that gravitates to a fruiting tree. Van Roosmalen recorded the activity under a fruiting *Brosimum* tree in Suriname, and I have seen the same phenomenon in Peru. When the crop of orange, cherry-sized fruits is ready, spider monkeys arrive in separate groups, squabbling over the available food supply. Much fruit is dropped, and it attracts seed predators, such as agoutis, acouchis, pacas, deer, peccaries, and birds like curassows and trumpeters, that destroy the seeds. Other monkeys eat the fruits but discard the seeds. Only the spider monkey carries the seeds away in its gut, and these seeds, defecated here and there away from the carnage around the parental tree, have a much greater chance of survival. The quetzal that flutters up, plucks an avocado, and regurgitates the seed at some distance from the parent tree has also successfully moved a seed encumbered by gravity and vulnerable to attack by assorted beetles. One suspects that a forest without wild avocados would soon lose its quetzals; likewise, it would be difficult to maintain healthy populations of these trees without quetzals or some equivalent, such as toucans. Just as jays, squirrels, and nutcrackers replant the oaks and conifers of the northern woods, quetzals, toucans, and spider monkeys replant tropical trees.

The importance of fruit in the tropical forest is also seen in the courtship and breeding behaviors of rainforest birds. A fruit is meant to be eaten. In this, it is distinct from animal prey. Fruit is so abundant that specialized frugivores are apparently able to get their fill with less effort than is required of insectivorous birds. David Snow, an authority on cotingids, first pointed this out when he argued that fruit abundance frees many male cotingids from parental obligations.

In the case of the fruit-eating cotingids such as bellbirds, the female rears the nestlings alone, with no assistance whatsoever from the male. In fact, the attendance of a male may actually be a liability for the female. If nest predation is high as a result of the large arboreal mammal and snake fauna, as is often the case, then extra traffic to and from the nest site may attract the unwanted attentions of predators. As a defense, many female cotingids build inconspicuous nests with only the number of twigs necessary to retain the eggs on a limb. Indeed, the nests of many species have yet to be discovered.

What, then, do male cotingids offer the self-sufficient females? The answer seems to be a good song and dance. On one of my trips into Peñas Blancas, I found a convenient overlook where I could stare down upon a bare limb that was used as the calling and courting perch of a male three-wattled bellbird. Like most fruit-specialist cotingids, the male looks far more ornate than does the female. Its snow-white head and neck contrast sharply with its chestnut body and most noticeably with the three black wattles, wormlike excrescences that dangle from the facial area. As I watched, the mousy, wattleless female landed on the perch beside the male. Immediately, the male flung his head sideways, flailing his wattles about excitedly. With a high-pitched whistle, he faced the female, his huge black-lined gape spread, and gave the famous loud bonk directly in the female's ear. He then leapt up, and she sidled toward the tapering end of the limb. Again, he flailed his wattles and leaned into the female, pushing her sideways as he whistled and bonked. She recoiled with the force of the sound, and they jumped up, leapfrogging over each other. The ritual was repeated, with the male pushing the female closer and closer to the end of the branch, until finally, he bonked her off. With the male in enthusiastic pursuit, she flew down, and I regrettably missed seeing whether his demonstration of auditory power, wattle wagging, and dance was suitably rewarded.

Bellbirds are far from unique. Many of the most conspicuous tropical birds, including cotingids, manakins, and toucans, are frugivores, a reflection of the fact that fruit is produced by 50 to 90 percent of the trees and shrubs in tropical rainforests. Animals that depend on fruit for more than half of their diet may constitute up to 80 percent of the avian and mammalian biomass in Amazonian forests.

In addition to abundance, availability and diversity are also in evidence. You will find different fruit during every season in the rainforest: strangely scented and beautifully pigmented fruits, fruits the size of cannonballs swelling on the sides of tree trunks or dangling on long ropy strands. Such fruits are never seen in markets, and they do not offer the conventional gastronomic enjoyment we associate with papayas, mangoes, and the like, species that have been improved by domestication. But for the naturalist, much of the pleasure of encountering a new fruit in the rainforest comes not from eating it but, rather, from inspecting and contemplating it and wondering about the role it plays in the lives of the birds and animals that make possible its propagation.

A male three-wattled bellbird displays to a female. She has to endure at a close distance one of the loudest calls of any bird.

Tails of glory
The ecology of prehensile tails

For several winters, I lived on a mountain slope in Costa Rica in a house that seemed designed for the armchair contemplation of wildlife. The large veranda overlooked a swath of cliff-edge forest that was well used by laughing falcons, variegated squirrels, and other animals, all of which provided nice accompaniment to a cup of coffee at dawn or something cold at the end of the day. The experience was enriched by the proximity of a large, spreading *Inga*, an umbrella-shaped leguminous tree that reached out to touch one side of the veranda. The *Inga*'s white powder-puff flowers drew steely-vented hummingbirds by day and their nocturnal counterparts, the large, long-tongued sphinx moths, by night. When the flowers had completed their pollination duties, big, green-golden, velvet-coated bean pods began to form. As they fattened and ripened, the pods attracted white-faced monkeys that would split them open, suck off the sweet white pulp, and spit out the beans, just as evolution had intended. To my chagrin, though, the white-faces, among my favorite primates, were often beaten to the pods by less welcome, musty-smelling nocturnal porcupines.

The porcupines are seed predators rather than dispersers, and they often use their incisors to neatly slit and empty every pod before it is ripe. Harvesting this bean feast is no mean accomplishment for the porcupine, since *Inga* pods usually form right at the tip of the limb in spots where the flowers are accessible only to hovering pollinators. No temperate-zone porcupine could ever perform such acrobatics, because it lacks the crucial adaptation of its tropical relatives: a prehensile tail.

A mantled howler monkey uses its prehensile tail to help it reach the flowers of a leguminous tree. Its tail is capable of supporting its entire body weight.

The prehensile-tailed porcupine, like many neotropical mammals, achieves its arboreal life with the assistance of what is, in effect, a fifth limb. A prehensile tail is, by definition, one that is able to grasp and to support the full weight of its owner. The tail of this porcupine species enables it to dangle from those thin branches denied a normal quadruped and so reach all of the *Inga* seedpods.

This particular adaptation has its disadvantages. To be an effective coiling, grasping organ, the porcupine's prehensile tail must be relatively thin and naked. By contrast, the tail of the North American porcupine is stout, well furred, and armed with special barbed quills. The defensive force of that organ must be felt to be believed. I had always wondered how dogs, merely by biting at a porcupine, were able to get the quills embedded so deeply in their flesh. I thought that perhaps the quills quickly worked their way in ratchet-style, as the barbs caught and were pulled deeper into the dog's twitching facial muscles. But recently, I had cause to chase a browsing northern porcupine out of the garden. The porcupine responded by raising its hackles, forming a crest of quills along its back to defend its vulnerable head region and turning its rear end toward me, as it waited for me to come to my senses. It was dark, and the mosquitoes were feasting, so I decided to prod the porcupine along by poking it with a plastic bucket. Instantly, its tail flailed around with the force of a strongly swung cudgel. The strength of the blow knocked the bucket out of my hand. I finally understood that the tail itself is capable of driving quills more than an inch into the body of a predator.

Given this physiological weapon, it takes a specialized predator with unique behavioral and physical adaptations to eat northern porcupines. The fisher weasel, one of the only northern porcupine specialists, uses rapid, darting bites to attack the forehead

As it travels through the canopy, the prehensile-tailed porcupine (*Coendou mexicanus*) browses on leaves, flowers, and fruit. The spine-free underside of its tail enables the porcupine to grip branches securely when foraging precariously on thin branches.

of its prey, while the great horned owl on a daytime foraging expedition will sometimes spear the northern porcupine with a talon through the eye socket. By contrast, all manner of unspecialized predators, including eagles, cats, and assorted weasels, eat the more acrobatic but less well-defended prehensile porcupine.

Nonetheless, the prehensile tail enjoys a broad currency, perhaps because most mammals do not customarily use their tails for defense. Normally, a tail's function is to assist balance, and the prehensile modification is thus not a costly option as far as survival is concerned. That does not mean the evolution of a prehensile tail has come without a price. The howler monkey tail, for example, represents about 6 percent of the howler's total body weight, a significant investment in muscle. To get an idea of what proportion of the body 6 percent represents, consider that the huge tail of the kangaroo accounts for only 4 percent of its body weight. The tail of a howler monkey weighs as much as one of its legs.

Anatomical studies show that prehensility is much more than simply increased muscle mass. In effect, it is a major rewiring of the nervous and locomotory systems. To graft a fifth appendage onto a mammal that for millions of years had propelled itself with four limbs must have required a long, slow process of evolutionary mutation and selection.

It is somewhat surprising, then, that so many unrelated, tree-dwelling neotropical mammals have evolved these tails inde-

pendently. Prehensile-tailed porcupines are joined by edentates such as tamanduas and silky anteaters, many species of opossums, some but not all monkeys, and, finally, kinkajous, which are members of the raccoon family and the order Carnivora.

Although the prehensile tail is often cited as evidence of extreme arboreal adaptation, many mammals manage to live in trees without this device. Squirrels get by nicely without it, as do most monkeys, coatimundis, tayras, and other long-tailed mammals that do a good deal of climbing. It is not merely the treetop life that favors these organs. The porcupine in the *Inga* tree offers as good an explanation as any: foragers that go out on thin limbs seem to have the greatest need for a prehensile tail. Enhanced feeding efficiency in the precarious outer reaches of tree crowns is made possible by the greater reach and security of the tail grip. Aside from sloths, few mammals are able to reach beneath their perch, but prehensile tails vastly extend the opportunities.

Primatologists have calculated that New World monkeys using prehensile tails increase their feeding sphere by 150 percent over animals that must feed in a sitting or standing position. That is especially true for those species that eat fruit and freshly flushed leaves positioned at the tips of branches. Spider monkeys, for example, which eat a great deal of fruit, new leaves, and flowers, have a tremendously well-developed prehensility. One can observe the large monkeys confidently feeding more than 150 feet (45 m) above the ground, hanging only by their tails. It is hard to explain the disconcerting, almost queasy feeling evoked in a human—this one at least—when a spider monkey is first observed in this seemingly reckless, death-defying, dangling position. One can easily accept a handhold as reliable and right behavior for a monkey. But seeing a large monkey suspended on high by only the end of its tail is so foreign to the sense of human security that it is rather like watching someone standing too close to the edge of a sheer cliff.

Other monkeys with tremendously thick prehensile tails are the howler and the woolly, and this is in keeping with their similar foraging strategies. Like spider monkeys, a howler can often be seen suspended by its tail, a technique that enables it to hang underneath a thin, bending limb and reach forward with both hands or even its feet to grasp the leaves, flowers, and fruit at the very tip of the limb. The howler also uses its tail as a convenient organ for descending from limb to limb, lowering itself several feet before dropping on all fours. By contrast, the related *Cebus* (capuchin) monkeys, which feed primarily on animal prey, especially insects, have only a semiprehensile tail. Rather than investing in tails that enable them to feed on fruits and leaves, they have developed keen vision and extremely dexterous hands. Frugivores such as spider monkeys have less need for a sophisticated, prey-catching hand; in fact, their hands, by comparison, are remarkably simplified.

The first time I held hands with a spider monkey, I was astonished to find that it had no thumb but just four long fingers, extensions of the spidery style of the rest of the arm and wrist. Only the feet have an opposable digit. That characteristic, so different from the *Cebus* monkeys, seems to suit spiders to brachiating, that is, swinging through the canopy arm over arm—a rapid and efficient method of getting from one fruiting tree to another some distance away. Brachiating is facilitated by the fact that the spider monkey's hand has fingers that point the same way and are of a similar length; also, it has no awkwardly splayed thumb to snag in passing vegetation. And when it is finally sitting still, the monkey uses its strong, dexterous prehensile tail rather than an opposable gripping hand to hold it securely.

Spiders seem to be the favorite pet-monkey species in Latin America, and on occasion, I have had one of these often lonely captives seek out social contact. It is a little unnerving to have a large adult black spider monkey sit beside you and use its candy-cane-shaped tail to reach up above its head like a hairy tentacle and grab your arm. The naked skin of the undersurface of the tail tip is pinkish, rough, and heavily lined, similar to the padlike skin on the soles of human feet. Its sensitivity is obvious; a spider seems to dislike having its tail tip touched.

The impact of the tail on monkey foraging has made me suspect that the presence or absence of a prehensile tail makes all the difference between closely related species in other mammalian families. Kinkajous and olingos, for example, are extremely common and closely related procyonids (members of the raccoon family) that have overlapping ranges and can sometimes even be seen in the same trees. Except for the bizarre red and giant pandas of Asia, procyonids tend to be omnivores with a preference for animal protein. However, kinkajous and olingos differ in ways that seem to reflect the role of the prehensile tail. Both animals are furry and elongate with a long tail and abdomen; the

The Central American spider monkey is highly mobile and ranges widely in search of fruit and other high-energy food. Its dexterous tail acts as a fifth limb, enabling it to dangle at the very tip of branches, where flowers and fruits are located.

One of the most common arboreal mammals, the kinkajou, top left, is among the few carnivores that have specialized in a predominantly fruit diet. Its prehensile tail allows it to make greater use of its forelimbs for plucking and handling fruit. While the closely related olingo, bottom left, lacks the prehensile tail typical of the kinkajou, it, too, is able to move quickly through the canopy, using its tail as a balancing organ.

olingo's tail is furred in a ghostly gray color, the kinkajou's in a rich honey-gold or brown. The latter has a blunt, almost catlike face compared with raccoons and coatimundis, a characteristic the olingo retains only slightly. The kinkajou is a bit heavier, but both animals are agile; their narrow shape enables them to walk nimbly along tree limbs in the dark. Yet of all the species in the order Carnivora, only the kinkajou has a prehensile tail and only the kinkajou seems to be a specialized fruit- and nectar-eater.

The olingo, by contrast, while it will eat fruit, moves about much more and also eats small animals—nestlings, mice, and the like—whenever it can catch them. It is tempting to believe that the high fruit-nectar diet of the kinkajou is facilitated by its prehensile tail, while the more predacious olingo forages over a great range and uses its tail for balance when striding along the tree branches. As with monkeys, the prehensile tail seems to be associated with a feeding strategy of herbivory and especially frugivory, while the more carnivorous forager retains the tail's conventional use.

The most arboreal of all opossums have well-developed prehensile tails, especially when compared with the shrew opossums, otherwise known as short-tailed opossums. Like the more northern shrews that just barely reach into the tropics, shrew opossums are highly insectivorous. But the woolly opossums, with their long prehensile tails, are specialists that live in the canopy and feed on flower nectar and fruit.

Generally, however, it is not a reliance on a diet of flowers, leaves, or fruit but simply the engineering required to forage in the treetops that seems to determine the prehensile-tail adaptation. Terrestrial edentates, such as giant anteaters and armadillos, lack them, while the mainly arboreal tamanduas and silky anteaters have strong prehensile tails. The silky anteater clamps onto stems and branches with both hind feet, using its tail to make a tripod and thereby freeing its forelimbs to slice open stems in its search for ants. The tamandua uses its tail as a secure holdfast that allows it to pull its foreclaws through the sturdy carton termite nest and tear away large chunks. The need for this rear-end support during foraging perhaps explains why the tamandua's ecological counterpart, the pangolin of the Old World, also has a prehensile tail.

Some snakes, especially Asian pythons and neotropical boas and vipers, also depend upon their prehensile tails to anchor them. This fits in well with their great degree of arboreality and the need to hold fast while handling large prey items. Terrestrial *Bothrops* vipers like the fer-de-lance do not need such a device, while arboreal *Bothrops* species, on the other hand, make use of it to hang onto a branch while biting a bird or lizard and to afford themselves greater mobility when descending from branch to branch.

But foraging mobility is not the only advantage of prehensility. Small arboreal mammals require a well-insulated nest, and it is not hard to imagine the difficulties involved in transporting nesting materials along the narrow limbs of tree crowns. A prehensile tail can be of great help; I have watched captive pregnant female marmosa opossums collect large tail-loads of fluffy cotton nest insulation and carry them to their nest sites. I have no doubt that they do this in the wild as well with kapok and other fine materials.

Prehensility's only illogical quality seems to be its geography. Prehensile tails are concentrated in the neotropics and are nearly

Like other small, light monkeys, the Central American squirrel monkey lacks a prehensile tail. It ranges through the lower and middle levels of the forest, running and jumping through the vegetation with great agility, searching for insects and small fruits.

absent in the rainforest mammals of Asia and Africa. Instead, many Southeast Asian rainforest animals move about by gliding between trees. The gliders include seven genera of squirrel, the flying lemurs (or colugos), frogs, two genera of gecko lizards, *Draco* lizards, and even snakes in the colubrid genus *Chrysopelea*. All of these animals have adapted so that their horizontal area is increased. All of them move between trees by climbing to a high point, leaping outward, and sailing down to another tree trunk. The mammals use lateral skin folds that they stretch out; lizards, frogs, and even snakes are able to flatten their bodies and assume a concave-belly profile as they hurl themselves from tree trunks and glide steeply down and away. That sort of locomotion is probably used regularly by foraging mammals, but I suspect that lizards, frogs, and snakes employ it more often as a device to flee nongliding predators. Gliding is rare in the African tropics and completely absent in the American tropics, a distribution made even stranger by the fact that we have gliding squirrels in North America.

That prehensile tails are rare in Asia and Africa is either an evolutionary accident or a consequence of differences in the environment on each continent. Mammalogist Louise Emmons

and botanist Al Gentry favor the latter view and suggest that the nonrandom distribution of prehensility reflects fundamental differences in the structure and architecture of tropical forests and trees on different continents. The Southeast Asian rainforest is relatively tall and liana-poor; Africa is liana-rich; and South America, intermediate in liana density, is distinguished by a high density of palms, which have a slippery leaf surface. Emmons and Gentry also suggest that the branches in neotropical forests may be more fragile than those in African or Asian forests and that these structural differences in turn favor different methods of locomotion. Thus mammals glide in Asia, use their prehensile tails in the New World, and resort to conventional means of locomotion in the purportedly easy-to-navigate African rainforest.

Not all tropical ecologists are enamored of this theory, however, and as an alternative, one might wonder if there is something about the faunal composition and histories of the regions that better explains the differences. Southeast Asia is rich in squirrels, bats, and rats, and perhaps they do well enough without a long suspensory device. But why don't some neotropical animals glide? In Asia, there are plenty of large leaf-eating primates that

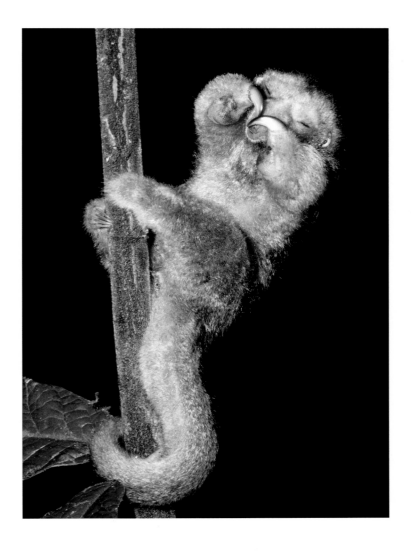

seem to have needs comparable to those of howler monkeys. Instead, the virtually tailless gibbon, for example, hangs from a branch by one long arm and forages with the other. That seems to give it about the same reach as a spider or howler but at the price of dexterity. Lack of evolutionary opportunity may best explain why most Asian animals do not have prehensile tails.

Although gliding makes much sense in open, liana-poor forest in parts of Asia and in Australian scrub (just as prehensile tails make sense in the neotropics), the lack of prehensile tails in Africa and Asia—and the absence of gliding neotropical mammals—seem inadequately accounted for by the slippery-palm/fragile-branch/liana-frequency theory. As always, it is easier to explain the presence of a trait—or at least to observe its adaptive uses—than it is to account for the absence of a characteristic, the reasons for which may be lost forever in undocumented history.

The issue of the strange biogeography of prehensility, then, hangs unresolved. That there ought to be a general explanation for it, we have no doubt. At the most fundamental level, though, this skillful tail, like most adaptations, comes from that universal drive to have one's reach exceed one's grasp.

The prehensile tail of the white-faced capuchin monkey, far left, is not as well developed as in heavier monkeys, so it is used mainly for additional security and balance.

The prehensile tail of the silky anteater, above left, is used as an extra support, freeing its forelimbs, which are armed with a huge claw, to defend itself or rip open small branches in search of ants.

Like many other arboreal vipers, the golden eyelash viper (*Bothriechis schlegelii*), above right, has a prehensile tail that it uses as an anchor.

Salts of the earth
Nutrient cycles in tropical forests

The field biologists working at Cocha Cashu, a research site in the heart of the Manú park in Peru, all wash their clothes at the same laundromat. This facility consists of a scrub brush, buckets, and a board nailed horizontally to a tree at the edge of the encampment clearing. They toss into the clearing the soapy rinse water collected in the buckets. One season, to the surprise and amusement of the biologists, a red howler monkey descended the washboard tree and proceeded to feed on the soil contaminated by rinse water. The biologists christened the howler "How Weird," because it became addicted to the practice. Not only would How Weird come down from the treetops to eat the soil that had been soaked in wash water, but he would also follow some of the biologists about, perhaps recognizing them as sources of particularly nourishing or flavorful exudates. Later, in a demonstration of primates' capacity to pick up on a good thing, another, younger howler, known thenceforth as "More Weird," showed up and likewise became fond of eating portions of the laundry area.

This was not an isolated incident. Rounding a bend along the Manú River, I was once startled at the sight of a troop of red howlers (which, incidentally, are strikingly large monkeys with long, rusty fur) down on the riverbank right at the water's edge. Normally, howlers, like all neotropical monkeys, stay up in the trees. They fear the ground and open spaces and are extremely loath to leave the safety of their treetop haunts; at the sight of danger, their response is to move higher in the tree. On the beach, however, the howlers were exposed and bizarrely out of

place. Stranger still, they were bent over, heads down, eating mud. Only with reluctance did they abandon their feeding stations and retreat, casting baleful glances over their shoulders as they shambled back into the vegetation.

Since these were absolutely wild monkeys, it seems clear that something vital must have been present in the soil to induce them to risk possible attacks by jaguars, pumas, ocelots, or humans. The most obvious explanation of the howlers' behavior is that it was an attempt to remedy mineral deficiencies in their diet. In the case of How Weird and More Weird, the attraction was probably the residue of sweat, bacteria, and exfoliated human skin mixed with phosphate-rich detergent. Such elements as nitrogen, phosphorus, potassium, and the like, are in notoriously short supply in many tropical soils as well as in the vegetation itself.

The interesting feature of howler geophagy, or earth-eating episodes, is that the chosen soil comes from particular spots. Monkeys and other mammals observed under more natural conditions have likewise displayed an appetite for ant and termite mounds. A study of the earth-eating behavior of monkeys in the Bornean rainforest revealed that these normally vegetarian monkeys never eat soil from the forest floor. Instead, they break pieces off termite mounds, which contain much less aluminum and much more calcium—four to eight times as much—than do forest-floor soils in the same area. Mammals such as elephants will also eat termite mounds, and my friend Phil Hazelton tells me that in Paraguay peccaries like to munch on leaf-cutting ant mounds.

Ant and termite mounds are probably appetizing because they are relatively rich in those mineral salts that the soil lacks. A little reflection on the life of an ant mound or a termite hill makes sense of this. *Atta* leaf-cutting ants represent a massive nutrient-concen-

Leaf-cutter ants (*Atta* sp.) carrying leaf fragments to their nest, where they are used for the cultivation of fungal gardens.

The underground nests of leaf-cutter ants are often enormous, harboring several million workers. Detritus removed from the colonies by workers accumulates outside, creating nutrient-rich soil in nest areas.

tration device. Such colonies are often huge, containing up to two million workers in their mature state. Each day, they travel along half-yard-wide (0.5 m) trails created with remarkable efficiency, radiating from the central mound area and leading for hundreds of yards into the forest. The ants lay down compounds that act as amazingly effective chemical signposts that direct the traffic. Along these trails, workers of various sizes issue forth to cut and carry home vegetation selected according to its chemical characteristics. Within the colony is a fungus garden that feeds on these plants. Because the fungus is in turn eaten by the ants, vegetation with secondary compounds that inhibit fungus growth is avoided. The fungal culture is groomed by a tiny caste of workers that manufactures and applies a variety of chemicals: a hormone that regulates fungal growth, a spore inhibitor that prevents invasion by foreign fungal spores, and a bactericide that eliminates bacterial contaminants. With such efficient management, a colony can harvest and process some 110 pounds (50 kg) of greenery per day, as much as does a good-sized cow.

Beside each colony, a trash heap develops, composed of old fungal substrate and the bodies of workers that have served their time. Over the years—decades, in some cases—nutrients build up. The mounds represent the residue left from the collection and digestion of literally tons of vegetation. Analysis of *Atta* mounds shows that they are significantly higher in soil nutrients than are surrounding forest soils. Where good drainage permits, the nests may go down several yards. The excavations of the workers bring fresher, less weathered soils to the surface, and the result is a virtual mother lode of fertility.

Invertebrates are also attracted to certain patches of soil. From time to time, one comes upon butterflies sipping at tropical soils along the banks and bars of the Manú River. As one approaches, the cluster looks like a huge dab of oil paint that suddenly explodes. Fragments of iridescent pigment fly into the air. Flecks of concentrated brilliance—sulphurous yellows, glowing oranges, gleaming whites, and sunset reds—all dip and dive evasively. They swirl round and round like a cloud of living confetti. The vivid, nervous creatures soon settle back to earth together. The *Phoebis* butterflies, swallowtails, sulphurs, *Urania* moths, and other legions of Lepidoptera land and move ahead, probing with their long proboscises for a taste of something in the sand. Still nervous, sometimes hopping and starting up, they press in, jostling each other, crowding, seeking some invisible essence that seems to be in a single particular spot. What attraction has them clustering and drinking so earnestly?

Remarkably, there seems to be only one study of what puddling butterflies are pursuing. Swallowtails in New York State are known to puddle where sodium exists in concentration. However, some other element must be a factor in luring certain butterflies. In Costa Rica, hordes of charming black, yellow, and white pierid butterflies (*Eurema diara*) gather around puddles in blankets. I have seen tight crowds so determined to continue drinking that a hungry Creole chicken could dislodge them only as it walked in their midst, snatching them up with each peck while the others rose up only to settle quickly down in the chicken's wake. *Eurema* can be seen streaming along the coastline, ignoring the

Leaf-cutter ants come in several sizes, and it is the median workers that do most of the leaf collection. The smallest workers, called minims, do much of the basic work in the colony, tending fungus gardens and larvae. They also ride "shotgun" on leaf fragments carried by larger workers, providing protection against parasitic flies.

sodium-steeped sands; in the tropics, I suspect that sodium is not always the nutrient of attraction for butterflies.

It was the great explorer and scientist Alexander von Humboldt who first reported that tropical people were also inclined to eat soil. In his travels in the American tropics at the end of the eighteenth century, he often observed native tribes eating dirt. A century later, Henry Bates, traveling on the Amazon rivers, observed much geophagy and remarked that "most people in the upper parts of the Amazon have this strange habit, not only Indians but negroes and whites. It is not, therefore, peculiar to the famous Otomacs of the Orinoco, described by Humboldt, or to Indians at all, and seems to originate in a morbid craving, the result of a meagre diet of fish, wild fruits, and mandioca meal." Odoardo Beccari, the great Italian naturalist who worked in Borneo, noted that his Dyak helpers, in good health and eating a bland diet, would nonetheless carefully select greasy clay stones from certain riverbeds and would eat them with zeal. The correlation between earth eating and the human diet is primarily a nutritional one, arising from the low-protein diet characteristic of marginalized tropical cultures. There seem to be no records of earth eating by highly carnivorous groups of humans or other species.

In various parts of Amazonia, areas of clay known as *colpas* can be found. At Cashu, there are several spectacular examples. Early in the morning, flocks of macaws begin to circle overhead, landing eventually in treetops overlooking the *colpa*. More than a hundred may settle, and the tree crowns fill with reds, blues, greens, and yellows, color patterns as brazen and bold as any ever seen on Earth. But the macaws are anything but bold. They constantly scan the *colpa* area and watch the sky for eagles. It may be hours before the first pair works up the confidence to descend. During the wait, the birds pass the time socializing, play-biting at each other with their massive shearing bills, turning somersaults on the limbs, dangling by one foot, and screeching raucously. When they finally fly down from the tree, they land on a very specific part of the bank, clinging awkwardly with their feet and flapping their wings for balance while they scrape off and swallow a seemingly full meal of clay.

It is somewhat curious that of all the birds found in Amazonia, it is the parrots (especially macaws) and the guans that eat clay. Ecologist Charles Munn, who studied macaws in Manú, saw fifteen species of parrots, including five different species of macaws, eating clay at *colpas*.

Rainforest butterflies like these pierids often gather in large, colorful aggregations on river banks, seeps, and other damp areas. Biologists suspect that the butterflies are drinking the fluids found there in order to absorb calcium or other mineral salts.

Perhaps it is something about the feeding ecology of the birds that predisposes them to geophagy. Their regular diet is fruit and seed crops. Macaws, in particular, are seed predators rather than dispersers and often attack unripe pods and fruits that are not ready for dispersal by other birds and mammals. As a result, macaws must somehow detoxify the defensive chemicals that plants employ against seed predators. The giant parrots are able to ingest the most unappetizing fare. I have watched them slice open the still green pods of *Hura crepitans*, a giant euphorb tree that is protected by a caustic white sap capable of raising red welts on human hide and blinding those unlucky enough to get the sap in their eyes. *Hura* is a well-defended plant that oozes a copious flood of this sap when cut at almost any point. It scatters its seeds with an explosive fracturing of the seedpod when it dries out. In order to feed on the seeds before they ripen and fall to the ground, macaws cleave the fist-sized green pods in spite of the sap. Macaws will also eat the bitter alkaloid-laden seeds of *Cedrela* trees.

Munn believes the macaw's diet of toxins explains its geophagy. He suggests that the clay eaten by the macaw serves to absorb the alkaloids found in its diet of seeds and fruit. It is well known that kaolin-type clays act as antidiarrheal medicine. Kaopectate, for example, is a popular clay-based product used for combating this disorder. The fine absorptive surface of clay buffers the digestive tract against excess fatty acids and probably absorbs toxins. Although the parrots admittedly have a difficult and demanding diet, I suspect that, in general, earth eating is usually a search for the mineral salts required by all herbivores rather than for a medicine.

Herbivores such as howlers and macaws may eat soil because fruit and leaf diets are low in minerals. One of the costs of eating foliage laced with defensive compounds is that in order to excrete the large toxic molecules, a relatively porous kidney is required. That, in turn, allows salts to escape in the urine. Temperate herbivores such as porcupines show a similar hunger for salts. They will eat your outhouse seat and chew your canoe paddle to shreds if you give them a chance, just because a sweaty residue of sodium is present. And like moose, they will wade out into ponds to forage for sodium-concentrating water weeds. By contrast, I know of no carnivore, temperate or tropical, that eats soil or uses salt licks the way herbivores do.

While salt licks attractive to game in North America tend to be high in sodium chloride, sodium is not, as we have noted, the salt of attraction in the tropics. It is not found in any concentration in termite and ant mounds. I have chewed at the *colpa* clay and found it to have a distinctly insipid and unsalty taste; there was no hint of sodium chloride. When Louise Emmons and a colleague analyzed this *colpa*, they discovered that it was high not in sodium but in calcium, an element that tropical soils generally lack. In fact, a hunger for calcium may explain most of the reported cases of geophagy.

Calcium is especially limited in level areas of central Amazonia, where there is little erosive potential and subterranean forces have failed to bring new mineral-rich rock to the surface. Soils of white sand are especially infertile. Some idea of how nutrient poor a hab-

In Amazonia, calcium-rich banks known as *colpas* attract macaws and parrots that travel great distances to collect and swallow the clay found there. The species seen here include red-and-green and scarlet macaws (*Ara chloroptera* and *A. macao*) at one *colpa*, above, and mealy, blue-headed, and orange-cheeked parrots (*Amazona farinosa*, *Pionus menstruus*, and *Pionopsitta barrabandi*) at another, right.

itat is and how effective is the nutrient sponging of the plants can be seen in the fertility of the runoff. Smaller streams and rivers in these areas have a characteristic black tint and calcium levels sometimes so low that analysts can get only a zero reading with their sophisticated equipment. In fact, plain rainwater contains twice as much calcium as does the river water, and what falls in the rain is obviously being retained very efficiently by the vegetation. The iron and aluminum content of the rivers is great, and their waters are, like peat bogs, highly acidic, with a pH of less than 4.5. Life in a calcium-poor environment has lead one species of snail to develop a shell constructed of a gluey secretion rather than the typical calcium-carbonate shell.

On land, the old, weathered upland soils are not seasonally inundated and are not enriched by silt. There, calcium levels also limit plant growth rates. The behavior of tropical tree roots is also an indicator of the importance of calcium. When bags of leaf litter are allowed to decay without contact between the litter and tree roots,

various elements disappear at differing rates. Sodium, potassium, and nitrogen leach away irrespective of root contact. But calcium and magnesium disappear much more quickly from a bag of litter with root contact than from one without. In effect, the roots mine the litter, sponging up the nutrients with great efficiency.

The absence of soil mineral salts such as calcium is one reason that clearing the forest and burning the slash to create cattle pastures is so unproductive; the bulk of the forest's fertility is held within the vegetation. Temperate soils may have a huge subterranean reservoir of fertile, nutrient-rich material, but in a tropical-forest system, as much as 95 percent of the fertile salts is held in the biomass of vegetation. When rainforest vegetation is cut and burned, the salts lie in a layer of gray ash on the surface of the soil. The first heavy rains leach away the ash, wasting most of the nutrient capital of this ecosystem.

The mineral salts that are left for the pasture plants are then exported at a great rate by agricultural harvesting. For example,

each 2,200 pounds (1,000 kg) of steer takes out of the system 59 pounds (27 kg) of nitrogen, 17 pounds (7.5 kg) of phosphorus, and 29 pounds (13 kg) of calcium. This degree of nutrient availability in a small area is simply not typical of tropical soils. Two hundred and fifty acres (100 hectares) of forest that once contained thousands of tons of biomass and nutrients is required to sustain a single steer. If ever there were a case of making a pathetic molehill out of a magnificent mountain, this is it.

More than a century ago, Alfred Russel Wallace, traveling through Amazonia, encouraged the conversion. "I fearlessly assert," he wrote, "that here, the primeval forest can be converted into rich pastureland, into cultivated fields, gardens, and orchards, containing every variety of produce, with half the labor and, what is more important, in less than half the time that would be required at home." Unfortunately, only the last element of his assertion has proved true. It is quick work to convert a complex forest into a simplified agricultural landscape, albeit an

Because rainforest plants absorb nutrients so efficiently, rainforest streams and rivers sometimes contain lower nutrient concentrations than does rainwater.

impoverished one. A couple of people armed with chain saws and matches can level and burn an astonishing amount of forest in a year. With a sixty-ton tree crusher, a single person can destroy 25 acres (10 hectares) every day.

The conversion of forest through felling and burning is often a one-way path that cannot easily be reversed by the successional process we are familiar with in temperate forests. After a forest fire in northern deciduous or coniferous forest, the vegetation surges back and the forest fills in rapidly. But in much of the tropics, the nutrients lost when rains wash away the ash are unrecoverable. Even if the organic matter of a northern forest soil is lost during a fire, each winter freezing brings up mineral rich rock and breaks it into soil. But the weathering of the parent material of the soil cannot replace the exported nutrients in most areas of the tropics. Old soils have had all the nutrient salts taken out of them. Indeed, some studies have shown that the nutrients in tropical forest that are lost to leaching and runoff are replaced not so much as a result of the weathering of the bedrock and soil but from atmospheric input—dusts and dissolved material borne by wind and rain. It takes some 230 years of rain to replenish salts such as potassium.

Many tropical soils contain a high concentration of aluminum and low amounts of calcium. Sometimes, the aluminum is so concentrated that the soil becomes bauxite, from which aluminum can be commercially extracted. That concentration of aluminum and depletion of calcium is particularly taxing for most rainforest tree roots, since aluminum prevents them from functioning. The plants that seem best able to deal with the high-aluminum/low-calcium situation created by soil leaching are the weedy tropical grasses. As a matter of fact, vast areas of the tropics in South America, New Guinea, and Southeast Asia have been taken over by huge monocultures of tough, virtually inedible grasses. Though neither man nor beast gets any use from them, they persist in a perverse form of perpetual ecological revenge.

Tropical regions are not strangers to the calamity that follows the massive disruption of a nutrient cycle. The destruction of tropical soils, accelerated by the development of agriculture, may have been responsible for the demise of some great city states. Tikal, Angkor Wat, and Palenque rose briefly in the midst of tropical forests and ended in ruins, thick with strangler figs. Some anthropologists believe that these cities exceeded the capacity of the surrounding land to supply their citizens with adequate food. Without efficient transport, it was impossible to import enough food to sustain the urban concentration of humans.

Yet in areas of poor tropical soils suitable only for growing rainforests, large cities are again growing up at a rapid rate. A few may someday become great and lovely, but most are so wretchedly out of balance with their surroundings that it is hard to imagine how they will ever escape the fate of Tikal and other similar civilizations. All of these cities are utterly dependent on the finite supply of fossil fuels to transport their food from distant lands as well as to produce the fertilizer needed to replace the salts of the earth now being lost. The cleared areas of land around these cities are largely incapable of meeting the needs of the people living at present in the regions of tropical forest.

Year after year, for thousands of years before the conquest, Amazonia supported as many as five million people. The thinly spread rainforest tribes were able to live off the interest without destroying the nutrient principal of the soil. The salts of the earth, scarce though they were, were just enough to sustain the system. The present and growing masses of people who have replaced the rainforest societies with denser agricultural and urban developments exist only through massive imported subsidies of food and fertilizers. It is impossible even to speak of a nutrient cycle in such a system, since the term implies some kind of internal equilibrium.

Explorer John Stephens wrote of Palenque: "Nothing ever impressed me more forcibly than the spectacle of this once great and lovely city overturned, desolate and lost, discovered by accident, overgrown with trees for miles around, and without even a name

The great Mayan city of Palenque and its temples may have been abandoned when local soils became too impoverished to grow enough food to support a large urban population.

to distinguish it." Perhaps when the fossil fuels give up, fertilizer is not easily produced and the flow of food resources is stemmed, then the modern cities and pastures that have supplanted rainforests will likewise become overturned and ruined. But if there are still trees to crack the façades and open the cement with their calcium-hungry roots, still lianas to drape and soften the hard angular walls, still bromeliads and orchids to flower on window ledges, and still macaws, peccaries, and monkeys to reclaim their territories, the spectacle will be anything but desolate.

Hermits & heliconias
The microcosm of plant & animal coevolution

Dropping down from the Atlantic side of the Continental Divide in central Costa Rica, the Peñas Blancas Valley is a gigantic slump of wet clay sprinkled with rock and slashed by mountain streams into slippery, knife-edge ridges and boulder-strewn ravines. The trail into the valley starts at the top with breadth and firmness, but in the center of the valley, it begins to narrow as it moves up and down successive ridges. Eventually, it branches and meanders into a vague network that seems to have been expropriated from nimble-footed tapirs. The trails demand one's full attention. There are nettles to rebuke the careless. Gravity conspires with greasy mud, and even with concentrated footwork there is an inevitable amount of slithering. In wet season, which here lasts for eleven months, the mixture of horse traffic and rain stirs up a viscous slop that may suddenly suck a rubber boot right off your foot. One thoughtless step, and you are mired, wobbling on one leg like a drunken crane.

Under such conditions, it is not easy to watch for wildlife. Happily, however, there is a long stretch where the trail is flat enough to set one's feet on autopilot and let the senses wander. The ever-present rumble of the river far below, the murmur of the feeder streams filtering through the mossy boles and tangles of vine, and the green shade make daydreaming possible. It was on this stretch some years ago that I came face-to-face with my first hermit hummingbird.

Out of nowhere, it cut through my reverie with a salvo of indignant squeaks. It delivered its high-pitched message and then

Heliconia burleana has long, curved flowers that allow easy access only to hummingbirds with long, curved bills, such as the tawny-bellied hermit, left. This minimizes the possibility of nectar and pollen being wasted on less specialized pollinators.

proceeded to spend the next few minutes inspecting me from various angles. Alternately, it approached and retreated, and as it hovered, it buzzed its wings loudly and flicked its long tail as though to call attention to its presence. I was able to admire at length the hermit hummingbird's bill, a tool gracefully but curiously curved, designed to weave one vital strand in a complicated web of ecological interactions. Then it darted away through the understory.

Wildlife watching in the rainforest is usually like this. The habitat does not offer panoramic spectacles. The words "tropical rainforest" may conjure up vistas populated by jaguars, brilliant macaws, and flowers amid the grandeur of towering buttressed trees. But the eager, expectant visitor is not regaled with the sight of charismatic vertebrates, gaudy birds, and luminous orchids. In the rainforest, close encounters with life that moves are usually rare but brilliant episodes; one is bedazzled for an instant and then left alone in the quiet greenery. Under such conditions, one must see the episode as part of a process; tracing the connections between organisms is the essence of rainforest appreciation.

There is a practical side to this approach that matches the habitat: you need hardly move your feet at all to go down many a long, convoluted ecological trail. If we follow the lead of the hermit hummingbird, it will take us directly to a spectacular, common, and important group of rainforest plants, the heliconias. The association between the hermit and the heliconia is, like many natural interactions, not an obligatory tie but, rather, a loose mutualism. Its curving bill allows the hermit to drink at and pollinate the flowers of many heliconia species. In turn, the heliconias play a major part in making life possible for the hermit. The two organisms are conjoined in a classic case of tropical coevolution that also sustains a vast subsidiary of other rainforest organisms. In

fact, if one wants to see truly representative rainforest wildlife, a patch of heliconias will serve as an ideal investigation site.

These members of the banana family (*Musaceae*) are among the most spectacular, abundant, and accessible plants of the New World tropics. Their bold, rhythmic forms seem drawn from a painting by Henri Rousseau, and like Rousseau's flat, two-dimensional renditions of tropical vegetation, heliconias often stand in dense, regal walls along the edges of forests and riverbanks. Heliconias grow as clumps or as umbrellas composed of huge leaves shaped like long, drawn-out canoe paddles several yards in length. Quintessentially tropical, they can afford larger leaves than any cold- or dry-climate plants. The leaves of some species are glossed with a waxy, silvery sheen, while others wear a purple tinge underneath. Their yellow-and-red flower bracts have a rigid, almost plastic solidity and a lively zigzag geometry—and may reach lengths of 6.5 feet (2 m), dangling in bold pendants. Some inflorescences erupt as heavy columns from the base of the plant; others stand erect in spiky fountains of color amid the greenery. The floral displays are designed to attract hummingbirds, and in lowland rainforest, if one wishes to watch these birds, finding a clump of heliconias is the best bet. Simply sitting nearby early in the day will be more rewarding than any amount of hiking.

The wedding of hummingbirds and heliconias is based on sex and energy. Like most plants, heliconias face the problem of transporting genes to and from other rooted individuals, but they require especially precise vectors for their pollen. Heliconias thrive where water and light are available to fuel their massive photosynthetic surfaces. In undisturbed forest, they are clustered in patches of light left by tree falls, along stream banks, and in seasonally flooded habitat. Broadcasting their pollen on the wind or using casual insect visitors is not an effective way to move their genes to other heliconias because of their habitat preferences and patchy distribution. A hummingbird is ideal for such long-distance pollen transfer.

There is a reciprocity between hummer and flower, a matching of form and function that is satisfying to behold. Like all birds, the hummingbird sees reds and other colors that insects do not perceive. The heliconia's bracts stand out like a bright flag against the green; they house the tubular corollas that only the long bill of a hummingbird can negotiate. In order to meet the energy requirements of its heat-radiating body, the hummingbird must daily drink up to eight times its body weight in nectar, of which heliconias produce a copious supply. As the hummingbird drinks from the well of nectar the plant holds at its base, one of two things happens: either the bird's bill or forehead is smeared with pollen from the plant's anthers, or the plant receives a fertilizing pollen load on its stigma from the laden bird.

The heliconia offers none of the sweet fragrance that lures bees and other insects to some flowers. In any case, like most birds, the hummingbird's sense of smell has atrophied. The heliconia's lack of scent and the elongated shape of its flower serve to exclude the swarms of unspecialized and less efficient insect pollinators. Many insects are catholic patrons of flowers and will visit dozens of different species, but the visit of a generalist pollinator has several disadvantages for a plant. An insect caked with flower

Heliconia inflorescences can be either pendant, as in the case of *Heliconia rostrata*, above, or upright, as in *Heliconia apparicioi*, right, both of which grow in the Amazonian rainforest.

pollen collected from half a dozen different species might clog the receptive stigma of the heliconia flower with useless types of pollen. A lack of selectivity by the flower visitor also means that any heliconia pollen the pollinator carries away may be likewise wasted in transfers to non-heliconias. In self-defense, the heliconia has evolved a flower that excludes such casual wastrels from its nectar, an energy-rich resource that is expensive to produce.

This exclusionary targeting is further enhanced by the fact that the pollen of most heliconia species is placed on a particular part of the hummingbird. As many as a dozen heliconia species may occur in one area, and an individual hummingbird might visit several during a single foraging bout. The anthers of each heliconia species have a particular length or contortion, thereby ensuring that the pollen adheres to a unique spot on the visitor's bill or face.

Most heliconias produce only a few open flowers per morning, and each flower lasts just one day, requiring the hummingbird to move from plant to plant. It is interesting to note that heliconias produce a surge of nectar just at the dim, cool hour of daybreak, when insects are quiescent but hummingbirds are making their rounds. That is the time to witness the actual match of bird to flower, the brief blur and buzz of wings, followed by silence.

The high metabolism of hummingbirds may also be important in allowing heliconias to climb mountains. I have always been impressed by the similarity in growth form between a marantaceous plant known as *Calathea insignis* and certain heliconias. Calatheas, which also grow in clumps and have large, paddle-shaped leaves, produce a conspicuous column of yellow flower bracts. At first glance, many people mistake them for heliconias. In Monteverde, Costa Rica, the two grow side by side on the lower slopes of the mountain. But as one climbs to 4,900 feet (1,500 m) and beyond, the calatheas diminish in abundance while the heliconias are as abundant as ever. I suspect the difference is that the heliconia enjoys a partnership with hummingbirds, while the calathea depends on bees for pollination. In the lowlands, the calathea is pollinated by a diversity of orchid bees, but at higher elevations, only a couple of species of large bees pollinate it, no doubt because only large bees are able to thermoregulate and fly at low temperatures. Hermits drop out at high-altitude cloud forest, but other hummingbirds have developed the hermit's form and foraging strategy; indeed, some sort of hummingbird can be found at all elevations in Costa Rica. Perhaps that is why heliconias extend nearly 3,300 feet (1,000 m) higher than do calatheas. (A calathea that does occur above 6,500 feet [2,000 m] in the Colombian Andes has evidently become modified for pollination by the hummingbird.)

These musings about hummingbird-assisted mountain climbing are speculation rather than scientific fact. But speculation is where the fun is, and much of the pleasure of standing by the heliconias watching a hummingbird blur and vanish is in imagining and wondering about the history and interlocked fates of plants and animals.

Other observations are much more verifiable. It is obvious that hermits are uniquely qualified to pollinate many heliconia species. Simply look inside the bracts, and you will find the curved flower tubes that cater exclusively to hermits. There is no substitute. Hermits offer more than just the right bill shape; they also have a foraging strategy that is conducive to this partnership. Unlike many short-billed hummingbirds, they do not defend a patch of flowers that they visit repeatedly. Hermits "trapline," moving from one clump of flowers to another, covering a circuit that may run for a mile or more through the forest. This means that hermits move pollen great distances with every foraging expedition.

Not aggressively territorial, hermits are easily displaced by other hummingbirds in contests over nectar sources. Ornithologist Gary Stiles points out that among non-hermits, control over a resource is usually size-related, with large hummers excluding smaller species. But even relatively large hermits are driven off by smaller, more aggressive non-hermits. The hermits survive because their unique curved bills allow them to exploit the specialized heliconia flowers that their straight-billed competitors are denied.

Such dependence may go back to the very origins of the heliconia. Not all heliconias are pollinated by hermits. Sometimes, non-hermit hummingbirds visit the shorter-flowered species. However, Stiles suggests that the non-hermit heliconias are more recent innovations. He points out that the geographic distribution of hermits and heliconias is closely matched and that the two organisms appear to share an ancient coevolutionary history.

Over time, such relationships act as resources that other organisms evolve to exploit. A number of hummingbird flower mites, all members of the family Ascidae, use hummingbird bills to carry them from one flower to another, where they breed and feed on nectar and pollen. The mites, too, bear witness to the evolutionary impact of the long hummingbird bill. Ecologist Rob Colwell notes that for their size, the mites run as fast as a cheetah, an attribute that equips them for the task of racing from lengthy flower to bill and into the nasal passages (or vice versa) in preparation for their voyage. They have only a brief instant to make the dash while the hummingbird hovers at the blossom. Colwell estimates that there are some five hundred species of hummingbird flower mites. Many of them show considerable specificity for certain species of flowers, including heliconias. Males may be armed with massive spines or raptorial legs that they use to crunch their rivals. If you dissect a blossom and use a magnifying glass to scan its interior, you may find these mites—tiny, pale, and obscure but tough and determined.

On a heliconia in Peru, I found what must be one of the richest assemblages of treehoppers, relatives of aphids. Treehoppers, or membracids, are attractive, if diminutive, sapsucking insects, noted for their weird appearance. Part of their exoskeleton, the pronotum, covers most of their body and is often sculpted into inexplicable shapes—balls and spikes, with pockmarked and pitted textures, striped, blotched, and polka-dotted in color schemes that range from the most cryptic simulations of caterpillar frass

Short-billed hummingbirds, such as the violet-crowned woodnymph, defend territories around clumps of heliconias with short, straight flowers, like this *Heliconia latispatha*.

Several species of tent bat, including these white tent bats, above, use heliconias as a roost site by day. The bats chew at the leaf veins on either side of the midrib, causing the leaf to fold down, creating a shelter from the sun and rain and reducing their exposure to predators.

Fresh, unfurling heliconia leaves provide a deep, protective funnel used as a shelter by animals such as this rufous-eyed stream frog (*Duellmanohyla rufioculis*), right, as well as katydids and other nocturnal creatures. The animal is hidden from predators and suffers less water loss than it would in an open resting site. The abode is only temporary and occupants are forced to relocate every three or four days as their leaf unfurls.

to bold blacks and oranges. Like many aphids, these insects often associate with ants and exchange services with them. The sap-suckers excrete sugar-rich fluids that the ants collect and eat, and the ants chase away such potential predators of membracid nymphs and eggs as ladybird beetles and mites. This community was located on *Heliconia metallica* flower buds and bracts. The membracids were tended by a dozen ant species, one of which was a very large, aggressive carpenter ant (*Camponotus*). Metalmark butterflies laid their eggs beside certain groups, and their caterpillars fed on the nymphs, placating the ants by exuding their own nutrient-rich pacifier.

Recently, I sent the Peruvian membracids that I had collected from this single species of heliconia to some taxonomists for identification. I had crude suspicions of the richness of the fauna, but I was astonished to get back the identified specimens and learn that these flowers were home to more than 20 species, including "*Anobilia luteimaculata, Mina* species, *Hemiptycha* species, *Walkeria* species, *Erechtia* species, *Tropidaspis* (several species), *Paragargara* species, a new undescribed genus near *Tropidaspis*, *Tropidolomia* species, *Amastris* species, *Horiola picta, Mendicea* or a genus near *Mendicea, Maturna* species."

Although the list may sound like Latinate gibberish, it is anything but that. It is a summary of great labor, the result of systematists gazing through microscopes until their eyes burn and sorting through drawers of specimens in dusty museum basements around the world, all in an attempt to organize the diversity. More than that, the list of names is a distillation of the incredible ecological diversity and ecological history inherent in the flowers of *Heliconia metallica*.

The bulk of the inflorescence of heliconias is not blossoms but the bracts that house the tubular corollas. There is more than mere advertising in such sturdy structures. The heavy bracts surround and armor the corollas, preventing stingless bees and other nectar-loving organisms from piercing the corolla through the side and robbing the flower of the sugary reward. Stingless bees, a ubiquitous presence in the tropics, have a knack for finding food, recruiting their nestmates with chemical trails and quickly chewing their way into the trove. The pressure of the nectar robbers is thought to be responsible not only for the heavy bracts of the heliconia but also for the fact that many of them grow upright and appear to have been designed either to catch rainwater or to hold water excreted by the plant into the cuplike bracts. The result is a moat that protects the submerged flower base from chewing bees. The watery defense, in turn, provides both housing and grazing to an entire community.

Such miniature ponds are duplicated throughout the rainforest in tree holes and crotches, in tank bromeliads and pitcher plants; in fact, one early student of the phenomenon described the upper reaches of the rainforest as a great aerial swamp partitioned into millions of tiny pools. The upright flower stalks of heliconias are part of that vast elevated wetland.

If you look inside a water-filled bract or perhaps tip its contents into a glass vial, you will find a miniature pond of aquatic life. A hand lens or reversed binoculars will reveal squirming mosquito larvae that prey upon protozoans, bacteria, and zooplankton. If

you are lucky, you will be able to spot even larger and more spectacular maggots, such as the rat-tailed syrphid or the larvae of the flower fly. These can be identified by a long breathing snorkel, a tube that extends twice their body length and allows them to breathe air while mining their way through the organic debris in the flower bract. At least one genus of rat-tailed maggot, *Quichuana*, is obligately tied to heliconia flowers.

The heliconias are probably evolutionarily indifferent hosts of the fly larvae, although there is a possibility that the larvae may enter the flowers and imbibe nectar. But there is no reason to believe that the heliconia's participation represents anything other than an incidental consequence of the evolutionary pressure exerted by nectar-robbing bees. Nevertheless, the flies have come to depend directly on the flower bracts in an ecological sense and to depend indirectly on the hummingbirds and stingless bees in an evolutionary sense. Such indirect, third-party links lend an intriguing and sometimes surprising quality to the study of each organism.

I find it interesting that a common genus of mosquito found in the water-filled heliconia bracts is the same group that has invaded the northern pitcher plants (*Sarracenia purpurea*), which grow in temperate sphagnum bogs. *Wyeomyia smithii* (a mosquito) evolved from residents of heliconias, bromeliads, and other tropical microponds and now spends half or more of its days frozen. We may look inside a pitcher plant or heliconia and reflect upon just how long and wide the connecting threads may run.

Some heliconia species with upright bracts, such as *Heliconia wagneriana*, above, house small aquatic communities—including mosquito larvae, which feed on the bacteria and small plankton that live in the water. Also visible here are the breathing tubes of syrphid fly maggots, reaching up from the bottom sediment where the maggots feed.

The owl butterfly (*Caligo atreus*), right, is among the biggest butterflies in the New World, attaining a wingspread of 6 inches (15 cm). Its caterpillars feed on the leaves of heliconias and often cause considerable damage. Note that this caterpillar, above, has been parasitized by a tachinid fly, which has laid more than twenty eggs on its back.

While some organisms find the heliconia a means to keep wet, others employ it in an effort to keep dry. I have often used its leaves as a makeshift umbrella, and many bats do so habitually. Tent bats cut the veins on either side of the large leaf's midrib with their teeth so that it folds down into a roost that is well protected against both torrential rain and baking sun. Honduran white tent-making bats will cluster under the leaves in groups of up to eighteen. The reasons for their choice of such conspicuous shelter remain a mystery, but it is clear that they must make a special effort to conceal themselves. Every day or two, they move on to another roost site.

New heliconia leaves form a protective cone-shaped tunnel that is used as a daytime roost by many nocturnal animals. Disk-winged bats enter at dawn and clamp onto the slick leaf surface by licking and applying suckerlike structures on their wrists and ankles. Fruit flies and earwigs are even more frequent residents. Sometimes, a frog is tucked inside the gradually unfurling, humid green cone. I once found in a heliconia tunnel a cone-headed katydid, a predator with antennae as long as its body. During its nocturnal feeding bouts, it leaves its antennae out; when a passing roach brushes against them, the katydid lurches forward, grabs the roach, and crunches it with its sharp, powerful mandibles. When I shook the katydid out of the leaf for a closer inspection, it bit my finger hard enough to gain its freedom. I consider it yet another mark of good wildlife interaction when you are able to get close enough to the objects of your curiosity for them to bite you.

The heliconia provides more direct sustenance to a wide range of insects that specialize in eating its foliage. The largest butterflies in the New World rainforest are the huge owl-eyed Caligos, which are as big as an open hand and wear large false eyespots on their wings to direct the strikes of birds away from their bodies. The caterpillars of this species often attack heliconias and banana plants.

If you look closely at the caterpillar, you may be able to chart the beginnings of yet another strand of dependence. Not all food chains terminate in the talons of an eagle or in the bite of a large cat. Some long chains follow a series of links ever smaller in size and much less obvious. Pasted onto the caterpillar's skin, you may find the eggs of tachinid flies nearly ready to bore inside. Once there, the larvae will tap the energy the caterpillar has taken from the heliconia leaves and the nutrients dredged from the soil and will convert them into flies. The labyrinth does not end there. Various ichneumonid wasps may then land and search out the parasitized caterpillar, using their long ovipositors to drill inside and lay their own eggs within the tachinid maggots. The final limit is reached when the ichneumons are in turn parasitized by tinier chalcid wasps the size of dust motes. Beyond this, the food chain belongs to viruses and microbes.

Chains and threads, pyramids and webs—the metaphors of ecology are not arbitrary. They express the labyrinthine and interwoven structure of natural communities. A naturalist may follow the strands from almost any rainforest plant and forever tread new ground, discovering novel tangles. The wildlife you seek is always right before you.

Termites & tamanduas
The role of wood eating in tropical ecology

They are creatures of interiors. Social but reclusive, all but a few shun the light of day, avoiding even moonlight. They live underground, in logs or sealed nests, and conduct their social lives within dark labyrinths often created and cemented together with their own dung—termites are nothing if not economical.

Numbering about 2,200 species, most of which are tropical, termites evolved from highly social cockroaches. Dependent on the digestion of woody material, termites have the remarkable ability to build a life entirely from wood. Colonies of some species thrive for years with nothing more than a chunk of wood from which to build their muscles, skin, nerves, mandibles, and minds.

Like subterranean beings the world over, termites tend to be pale and soft, save for the armored soldier castes that stand ready to venture out into the light to defend their colonies against invaders. The workers usually live retiring, sterile lives, forgoing reproduction and chewing their days away building the domestic empire of their parents. For this specialized role, they have evolved an aspect not unlike that of the modern dairy cow—their swollen bellies stretch glistening and taut over a massive gut of dark ferment.

Like the digestive systems of cows, those of termites are made possible by microbes. Several dozen species of protozoa and bacteria live within the intestines of termites and nowhere else. The microorganisms do the heavy enzymatic work of cleaving cellulose into usable sugars. The fact that the special microbes must be passed from parent to offspring by anal feeding to inoculate the newborn's sterile digestive tract probably explains why the ancestral wood-eating roaches began to live in extended family groups.

Their gut microflora give termites access to a huge resource base denied to other herbivores. Much of a rainforest is pillar after pillar of inert cellulose and lignin wrapped by a thin sheath of living, growing cambium and capped by a paltry 220 pounds (100 kg) or so of leaves; less than 2 percent of the rainforest is leaf matter. The bulk of the rainforest is tons of cellulose in the form of tree trunks and limbs. That cellulose is a reservoir of solar energy converted into chemical energy as carbohydrates.

Plants construct sugars as a store of energy, but the sugars can be repackaged in various ways. Sometimes, they are stored as a nutritious chain such as starch; more often, the solar energy ends up as cellulose.

Wood is composed of 60 to 70 percent cellulose and 10 to 25 percent lignin, a three-dimensionally branched polymer that stiffens cell walls, strengthens wood, and is one of nature's most indigestible molecules. Ecologist John Janovy gives a good summary of the functional significance of such molecules; as he puts it, "The human sits on a chair and eats a French fry." Tropical rainforest is full of material that is suitable for chairs, but only a small fraction of the forest is as digestible as a starchy French fry.

Lignified woody material can only be a profitable diet for low-energy organisms, such as insects. Indeed, the abundance of wood-eating insects, such as termites, in any tropical rainforest results in part from the special metabolic solutions required to digest woody matter. In general, only 3 to 10 percent of a warm-blooded animal's food intake is converted into biomass.

The northern tamandua is a major termite predator. It is armed with powerful claws and forelimbs adapted for tearing open nests, and its elongated mouth houses a long tongue with which it licks up termites.

Many termite species have soldiers with enlarged heads that have sharp, defensive mandibles. Worker termites, by comparison, have smaller heads with chewing mouthparts.

The Mexican burrowing toad (*Rhinophrynus dorsalis*) feeds almost entirely on termites. It spends most of its life underground, emerging only to breed after heavy rains.

The rest is burned in maintaining an active, warm-blooded body. By contrast, insects, which usually operate at air temperature, do not radiate much metabolic heat, converting about 60 percent of their intake into more insect. As a result, insects are more abundant than are mammalian herbivores. If the equations were otherwise, we might see huge mammals the size of the larger dinosaurs crunching entire tree trunks like stalks of celery. Instead, it is termites, along with certain beetles and fungi, that break down and transmute the wooden heart of the forest.

Fungi are perhaps the greatest competitors of termites because certain kinds—the bird's-nest fungi, for example—are able to attack lignified cellulose. A few termites have capitalized on this ability by becoming allies of the fungi. Lacking elements of the gut microflora that the lower termites use to digest cellulose, some higher termite species have begun farming mushrooms, growing them either on woody debris or on their feces and then consuming the fungus. This syndrome closely parallels that of the leaf-cutting attine ants, and it seems plausible that in many senses, it is an ecological equivalent. The leaf-cutting attine ants are exclusively New World, while the fungus-culturing termites have radiated most extensively in the Old World tropics.

Together, termites and their microbial and fungal partners recycle and convert a tremendous volume of the standing biomass of the rainforest, consuming deadwood on a scale compa-rable to the area devastated by forest fires in the North, beyond termite country. But the forest fire of the tropics burns in the anaerobic bowels of termites. It does not rage uncontrollably but is, instead, a slow, continuous burn, never allowing the buildup of litter and limbs that can ignite a whole forest at once and take it down to mineral soil and rock. And unlike fire, termites can themselves become the food of choice for many rainforest organisms.

Termite nests are sought as domiciles by various birds and bees, ecological evidence of the termites' dependable ubiquity. Even stouter testimony to the termite's value as a resource are those other insects that inhabit the nests in commensal or parasitic fashion. This array includes specialized flies, beetles, mites, and parasitoid wasps, many of which have become as bizarre as cave creatures with the hypogeal hallmarks of being blind, white, and puffy. A naturalist might easily spend a lifetime in the rainforest doing nothing but collecting and cataloguing the minuscule "guest" species living in termite mounds and never see the end of this esoteric labor. In fact, such people exist. As one might expect, they are devotedly enthusiastic about their eccentric mission. I have seen them in the field, eagerly crushing termite nests into sifters and extractor funnels, crowing in jubilation at the sight of their microscopic discoveries, the representatives of that dim troglodytic frontier of termite-nest interiors.

In a rainforest, the usual aficionados of termites include a number of ant species as well as assassin bugs that wait by the termite trails, picking off individuals that they impale and then suck dry of their vital fluids. Vertebrates that eat soil termites probably include armadillos and the Mexican burrowing toad (*Rhinophrynus dorsalis*), a swollen, oval jelly blob of a toad with tiny eyes, a small, pointed head, a mouth made for bite-sized prey, and short, shovel-like limbs suited to its moleish habits. Blind snakes and caecilians work underground and are also likely termite predators. But the most conspicuous predators are edentate mammals such as tamandua anteaters, which have evolved as consumers of termites and ants. This specialization is not surprising, since, collectively, ants and termites make up as much as 30 percent of the animal biomass in a tropical rainforest—an abundant, ubiquitous resource, if a bit acrid and chitinous.

Anteaters comprise four species in a single family in the order Edentata, which also includes the sloth and armadillo families.

The giant anteaters that range through savanna and rainforest can weigh nearly 90 pounds (40 kg). At the other extreme is the least known but potentially most abundant species, the silky anteater, a mere handful of golden fur that, at 10 to 18 ounces (300 to 500 g), weighs less than a respectable hamburger. A completely arboreal, nocturnal ant specialist, the silky anteater locates its prey in hollow twigs that it neatly slices open with its huge, scimitar-shaped foreclaws.

The neotropical naturalist will most likely encounter one of the two species of tamanduas, a common, intermediate-sized (as much as 13 pounds, or 6 kg) arboreal anteater with a thick, prehensile tail that equips it for treetop forays. Its diet includes more termites and fewer ants than that of the other anteaters. In the wet rainforests of Central America, the tamandua is marked with a bold, two-toned black and tan coat, whereas in South America, tamanduas are usually a uniform honey color. I have seen the latter, as they walk methodically along limbs, being followed

Like termites, cup fungi (*Cookeina tricholoma*) are able to digest dead wood, thereby playing a crucial role in the cycling of rainforest nutrients.

by clouds of tiny hovering insects, and I have often wondered if these followers depend on the tamandua to provide access to the heart of termite nests.

The tamandua has the same massive foreclaws common to all anteaters and powerful, seemingly pneumatic forelimbs useful for breaking open termite mounds. I once shared a truck ride across Beni in Bolivia with a tamandua I had caught in a plaza in San Borja, where it was being tormented. There was no alternative but to guide it into a woven sugar sack and take it out to the field. As I rode in a truck jammed with supplies and people, the sack rolled against my leg. I felt a strong pull and looked down, horrified to see a set of the long foreclaws reach through the bag, curve easily around my boot and tear through the rubber. Luckily, my boots were large, and I was only grazed by the passing claws. But I have no doubt that they could dig just as effortlessly through muscle and tendon. That strength is legendary: giant anteaters are said to have killed jaguars, and even humans who have harassed the anteater and gotten too close to its powerful embrace have met a similar fate. However, anteaters use their powerful claws primarily for opening termite mounds and ant colonies.

Once the nest is breached, the anteater uses its long, skinny tongue as a conveyor belt for hapless termites and ants. The giant anteater's tongue may extend 2 feet (60 cm) out from its noz-zle-shaped face, and the tongue sheath and muscles run all the way back to the breastbone. Lined with small, backward-pointing barbs and coated with sticky saliva, the tongue thrashes back and forth at a rate of 150 times per minute, whipping large quantities of termites back into the anteater's toothless mouth.

Termite nests are fixed and plentiful, but tamanduas and giant anteaters nevertheless range over a considerable area. It is interesting to note that tamanduas and their kin never seem to dent the termite population. Tamanduas damage only 20 percent of the nests within their range and rarely demolish a nest entirely. Could this be prudent predation, with steady, modest harvests that allow the termite population to recoup and sustain itself, which in turn ensures the tamandua a predictable food supply? Sensible as that might sound, such strategies are not evolution-arily stable against those competitors that "cheat" and go for short-term gain. A better explanation of the brevity of each feed-ing bout is the anteater's distaste for the masses of soldiers that begin to congregate at the breach.

Termite soldiers can be a formidable deterrent. In some cases, outright swordsmanship defends the colony. I once watched E. O. Wilson gingerly open a nest in the laboratory. He carefully lifted a section of nest carton, then suddenly yelped and pulled back his hand, with blood pouring from a neatly slit finger—the work of a single soldier's defensive slash. The larger soldier castes often have sharp slicing mandibles powered by the huge muscles that pack their bulbous, shiny, helmet-shaped head capsule. However, the termite's chemical defense is even more highly developed. A

Globitermes soldier is a living grenade. Glands fill fully half of its abdomen with a noxious, gummy secretion. When the soldier is confronted, powerful abdominal contractions spew the fluid out of the mouth, sometimes rupturing the abdomen; the soldier dies in a tangled mass, a self-sacrifice made in defense of its immediate kin.

Other termite groups have a similar stratagem. The carton nests of the *Nasutitermes*, one of the most common social insects in Latin America, can be seen attached to trees and vines everywhere. Some parrots, trogons, stingless bees, and various ants habitually use *Nasutitermes* nests as their own domicile, a dependence that again testifies to the predictable abundance of the resource. I have often walked through riverside forests and seen in a single glance half a dozen *Nasutitermes* nests, some as large as I am and each containing thousands of termites. One wonders, then, where the tamanduas are. There seems to be a glut of food for them. Are the tamanduas predator-limited, their numbers kept down by cats and eagles? The answer is probably "no." Termites are less easily captured than the abundance of the nests might suggest. The *Nasutitermes* colonies all contain a soldier caste with a dark, swollen head that bears a conspicuous spout, hence the name *nasute*. The nozzle-headed soldiers defend the colony by blowing sticky defensive compounds over intruders. The secretion can be easily collected by poking a finger through the flaky, crumbly nest wall. After the soldiers anoint the finger, it will smell of turpentine or some other piny resin.

These substances—called terpenes—issue from a huge head gland and from the specialized tubular head capsule, a modification that renders the soldiers of many nasutes unable to feed themselves; they must be fed by the workers they defend. The defensive investment in nasutes may be as high as 20 percent of the colony population. Apparently, the cost is worthwhile. Terpenes do not taste nearly as pleasant as they smell. Studies show that tamanduas prefer to feed on workers in galleries, where there are fewer soldiers than in the nest proper and where the king and the fecund queen reside.

The termite's defensive weapons prevent the tamandua and others from eating in peace, so the nest is not normally wiped out by anteaters or by raiding ants or hammering birds. The South African aardwolf, another specialized predator of termites, is likewise deterred. Once it exposes a colony, it will feed voraciously, but eventually the increasing numbers of soldiers arriving at the breach force it to move on.

Termites remain numerous enough to have a profound impact on the tropics, and their abundance has not helped their reputation. Explorer Alexander von Humboldt argued that "the termites (*comején*) create obstacles to the progress of civilization, in several hot and temperate parts of the equinoctial zone, that are difficult to be surmounted. They devour paper, pasteboard, and parchment with frightful rapidity, utterly destroying records and libraries. Whole provinces of Spanish America do not possess one written document that dates a hundred years back. What improvement can the civilization of nations acquire if nothing links the present with the past, if the depositories of human knowledge must be repeatedly renewed, if the records of genius and reason cannot be transmitted to posterity?" I have had the same horri-

Termites are an important part of the diet of the nine-banded armadillo.

Unlike its northern relative, the southern tamandua is variable in color. Individuals from eastern Brazil are almost identical to northern tamanduas, while those from the Guianas and northern Amazonia are typically pale blond. In some areas, both color forms occur along with many intermediates.

fied reaction upon opening a nice old book in a run-down house or field station and finding termite frass rather than wisdom.

More recently, termites have been castigated by climatological researchers who have identified them as major contributors to the greenhouse effect. The termite's metabolic process releases vast quantities of carbon dioxide and methane into the atmosphere. These gases, along with chlorofluorocarbons, trap the energy of sunlight that would otherwise reflect from the Earth's surface and radiate back into space. The greenhouse gases raise the temperature about 93 degrees *F* (34 degrees *C*) above what it would otherwise be on a planet without our atmosphere, which is a good thing and is ultimately what makes life possible as we know it on Earth. Unfortunately, greenhouse-gas increases are raising the Earth's temperature at an unprecedented rate. The resultant climate change threatens to wreak mayhem within this century by melting polar ice caps, which would in turn raise sea levels, submerge island nations and coastal civilizations, and devastate agriculture.

Termites have been targeted as compounders of the problem by preventing the buildup of a fixed carbon pool and by adding huge quantities of methane, a potent greenhouse gas. A recent estimate of the Earth's termite population placed it at about 250,000 billion (relative to humanity, this represents about 38,000 termites per person). But the biggest contribution to the greenhouse ef-

fect is not from termites. Human generation of carbon dioxide by burning fossil fuels and the burning of Amazonia are the greatest threats to the vast tropical carbon pool. The basin supports the world's greatest concentration of vegetable biomass per unit area, about 220 tons per acre (500 metric tons per hectare), which stores in a beneficial form a quantity of carbon equal to 20 percent of that now in the atmosphere. Burning this vegetation will raise by about 8 percent the total content of the atmosphere that is buffered by the oceans, an action that dwarfs the effects from termites. As it is, natural forests and termites exist in equilibrium.

Termites do produce methane in their anaerobic digestive process. Initially, it was suggested that termites might pump as much as 168,000 million tons (150,000 million metric tons) of methane into the atmosphere every year, about one-third of all the methane produced by decomposition and released from areas of permafrost and from the ocean. Later estimates have reduced the figure by an enormous factor. It now appears that the biggest agricultural contributor of methane is the huge 1.3-billion-strong global herd of flatulent dairy cows and beef cattle, thought to pump 112 million tons (100 million metric tons) of methane into the atmosphere annually. If you have ever stood behind a cow for long, you will appreciate the volume of gas it is capable of generating. Rice paddies may contribute a comparable amount. Dumps of human garbage are another huge source (when I lived

116

Termite colonies may contain hundreds of thousands of termites, a concentration of protein that attracts many specialized predators and parasites. The nozzle-headed soldiers of nasute termites (*Nasutitermes* spp.), seen here, defend the colony by spraying chemicals on invaders.

near Phoenix, Arizona, landfills of household garbage were constantly bubbling and often caught fire); the combined landfill output of methane may reach 77 million tons (70 million metric tons) a year. In any case, methane levels recorded in core samples of Antarctic ice show an exponential, skyrocketing increase that is expected to play a major role in global warming.

On the other hand, the biosphere has lived with the termite's gaseous contribution for many millions of years, and we may discount any suggestion that termites are in the same disruptive class as bovine-loving, gasoline-guzzling, profligate, proliferating humanity. In fact, termites may offer something of a counterpoint to the predicament in which we find ourselves. Termites are societies in a rough equilibrium with their biotic environment; they neither vanquish nor are vanquished, and they have evolved a vital role in the recycling economy of the forest. We have yet to have such an equilibrium forced upon us.

William Morton Wheeler, an eminent student of social insects, found much human significance in the ways of termites. In one of his many essays, he expresses the opinion of a wise old termite king, who explained that humans "could form a much better society than the present if you could be convinced that your further progress depends on solving the fundamental preliminary problems of nutrition, reproduction, and social defense which our ancestors solved so successfully in the Cretaceous . . . . If you only increase your biological investigators a hundredfold, put them in positions of trust and responsibility much more often and before they are too old, and pay them at least as much as you are paying your bricklayers and plumbers, you may look forward to making as much social progress in the next three centuries as you have made since the Pleistocene. That some such opinion may also be entertained by some of your statesmen before the end of the present geological age is the sincere wish of yours truly, Wee-Wee, 43rd Neotenic King of the 8,429th Dynasty of the Bellicose Termites."

To this, the tropical biologist of the present and warming day can say only "Amen."

117

The hidden
The adaptive coloration of prey & predators

In the rainforest, there are twigs that walk, leaves that leap, bark that flies, and masses of thorns that explode into fragments when touched. Or so it seems. The most abundant surfaces and structures of the forest—the bark, moss and lichen, twigs, dead leaves, and green foliage—are a template for elaborate concealment and sophisticated deceptions. Insects, frogs, lizards, snakes, birds, and cats find refuge by blending into the pattern and textures of the rainforest.

The large *Markia* katydid lives in the mossy, epiphyte-laden cloud forests of Central America and feeds on the masses of pale green, long-fibered *Usnea* lichens. While most katydids are decidedly smooth-skinned, *Markia* sprouts and bristles with protrusions that match the width and hues of the lichen fibers. Its net-veined wings, bristling legs and face, and even its striped eyes are all worked into an amazing simulation of lichen texture, tint, and form. The artistry of this katydid is so well drawn that it elicits exclamations of admiration from even the most experienced and worldly biologists. The ardent Darwinist holding such a fine beast in hand is both gratified and amazed at the craftsmanship wrought by the unthinking, impersonal force of natural selection. It is more than just the closeness of the match between cryptic organisms and their environment, however, that interests the student of rainforests. This art tells us something about the importance of predation in the lives of rainforest organisms; it is an exposition on the sense of sight. The art of camouflage is, by its nature, inaccessible. It is extremely difficult to stumble on cryptic organisms either by chance or by searching diligently through rainforest vegetation.

This well-camouflaged green leaf mantis (*Choeradodis rhombicollis*) is inconspicuous to both predators and prey.

The best opportunity is to inspect the area around a light at night or, better yet, to invest in an ultraviolet insect-collecting light. By morning, an assortment of insects that are virtually invisible in their natural haunts can be found clinging conspicuously to the walls.

Most of these will be moths that mimic either twig ends or dead leaves. The former have jagged gray and black tufts of scales that protrude from their forward region, simulating the broken fibrous end of a snapped twig. Rolled into a tubular shape, the wings conceal the abdomen, and the hidden legs reach back within the tube to grab the surface and tilt the body at an angle.

The most remarkable mimics of all are geometrid moths, which resemble dead leaves; any clue to the moth's existence is concealed. No legs, antennae, or eyes protrude; all are tucked beneath the wing surface. The wing edges curl up like a drying leaf, and the wing surface is drawn out to produce the pointed tip characteristic of so many rainforest leaves. Wing scales re-create the pattern of leaf veins, and against the drab brown wing surface, splotches of color faithfully imitate decaying fungi on a leaf surface.

For maximum appreciation, it is best to examine such creatures on their natural perches. Try searching a tree trunk near the light you have set up. A different group of moths will settle on these surfaces. The mottled greens and grays that seem so vibrant and conspicuous on a plain background dissolve into the speckled pattern of the bark. This disruptive coloration breaks up the outline of the body into areas of high contrast, and into shapes and lines that are distinct in themselves and whose geometry and configuration bear no semblance of the organism's total shape. The eye receives the light reflected from the bold, bright spots of pigment, but the mind cannot process and sort out the amorphous shape of the whole when it sits on a background of similarly contrasting hues.

The lichen katydid (*Markia hystrix*), shown above, lives surrounded by the *Usnea* lichen on which it feeds, and it has evolved spiny appendages and pronounced wing venation that mimic the lichen's appearance.

Stick insects are superb mimics of twigs, leaves, and other vegetation. This species, on the opposite page, found in Costa Rican cloud forests, resembles the moss that covers the branches among which it lives.

Context is everything to such moths, and studies have shown that they are capable of choosing a resting substrate that matches their patterning. Their camouflage follows the same principles as did the Renaissance painters of the great cathedral domes, who created the impression of humans and angels cavorting overhead and rising into the heavenly vault in an unbroken continuation of the ascending pillars and arches; no line or frame separates the art from its surrounding environment. So, too, the moth eliminates lines and borders. It flattens itself, wings flush with the surface, thereby eliminating any line of shadow. There is no outline, no silhouette, no three-dimensional quality to reveal the living object. A painter conveys depth on a two-dimensional surface with breaks and changes in width of lines. Within the surface of its wings, the moth pattern strives for the opposite effect. The color patterns of each wing overlap so that there is no separation of the pattern from forewing to

hind wing. The continuity of the swirls and patches of color obscures the moth's silhouette.

The mirror image created by the bilateral symmetry of the two paired wings is the only clue to the moth's identity. However, many resting moths will also contort their abdomens, twisting them awkwardly in what appears to be a deliberate attempt to destroy the symmetry.

Such cryptic adaptations are not without costs; those moths that modify their wings and body form make a large aerodynamic sacrifice. The huge investment these organisms make in invisibility suggests that they are highly palatable and desirable prey, which inspires the question: How do rainforest birds find these insects? The cryptic moth's anonymity is designed to thwart opponents at a distance, as is a soldier dressed in variegated battle fatigues. A bird that takes a wide view of a tree trunk or the forest floor, sweeping its glance up and down and back and forth,

actually sees many edible camouflaged organisms. But it "sees" them only in the sense that the retina of its eye absorbs the light reflected from the insects' bodies. The identities and locations of the prey go unrecognized, because the bird's brain is unable to process and categorize the many patterns of light.

The sweeping view of a predator is cluttered with sensory irrelevancies. Predators of large, active prey items can ignore more of the environment and react only to movement. But for birds that prey on cryptic and quiescent prey, a different technique is required. An array of New World rainforest birds like woodcreepers and leaftossers have evolved a means of exploiting the large numbers of camouflaged insects by acting like foraging temperate-zone nuthatches. By walking up and down tree trunks or reaching into rolled leaves and crevices, their field of view is restricted and they are brought into close contact with the insects that may reveal themselves by movement or tactile cues.

Cryptic insects persist in their deceptions even when prodded. When resting moths are touched, their response neatly matches their appearance. Moths that are not imitations of the inanimate will merely flutter off in a straightforward attempt at escape. But the most highly camouflaged species attempt to sustain their masquerades. The stub ends of branches shift just enough to get away, then pull down inert and rigid. The dead-leaf mimics simply let go and fall as a dead leaf would, sideslipping and whirling softly to the ground.

The worst thing a camouflaged organism can do is flee. Purposeful movement destroys the sham and provides visual predators with a stimulus and location for attack. But sometimes an organism is forced to move. If you are lucky enough to find a walking stick, give it a prod. It will slowly step away, all the while rocking back and forth in simulation of foliage vibrating in the breeze.

Upon discovery, katydids may hop, but they freeze upon landing. Tree frogs often do the same, leaping as far as possible, then instantly tucking in their feet, closing their eyes, and adopting their imitation of lichen on bark. Likewise, a pauraque—a cryptic night-active bird that nests and rests on the ground by day—will typically flutter upward only when it is almost underfoot, weaving in a looping swerve and quickly settling a short distance away, falling mothlike and silently back onto the litter. Many insects, especially dark, hard-bodied beetles such as weevils, simply curl up and drop when disturbed. The time required to scrutinize, prod, and poke each bit of litter makes it an unprofitable proposition, and the hunter moves on.

Credible imitation of the dead demands immobility during daylight hours, when many visual hunters such as frogs, lizards, mammals, and predatory birds sit and wait for camouflaged organisms to reveal their presence through movement. Not surprisingly, prey species that most resemble inanimate objects tend to be active at night.

The counteradaptation of some day-foraging birds is to use "beaters" to flush out the cryptic palatable insects. In Peru, I once watched a nunbird that seemed particularly interested in some machete work being done in a clearing. The coal-black bird with a stout coral-colored bill was perched on a clothesline, indifferent to my presence close by. I could see the glitter of its large eyes as it cocked its head one way and then another, peering, scanning; it bent and stretched its neck and hopped onto the wire to get a better view, all the while staring with rapt, unblinking concentration. The instant a cricket or katydid hopped or moved, the waiting nunbird pinpointed its new resting spot and swooped down to take it.

The nunbird was probably indifferent to my presence because it is accustomed to associating with large mammals, includ-

In form, color, and texture, these moths (Notodontidae), above, perfectly simulate two broken twigs.

The spiny body of the thorn bug (*Umbonia spinosa*), left, resembles a thorn, a disguise that may deter predators.

These two geometrid moths mimic the pattern of dead leaves on the forest floor. At rest, these insects are almost impossible to detect without careful searching at close range.

ing peccaries and possibly monkeys. Just as cattle egrets congregate placidly around cattle and horses in order to harvest the pasture insects the herd kicks up, many rainforest birds traipse after mammals.

In Costa Rica, I have watched forest-falcons and double-toothed kites trailing troops of white-faced capuchin monkeys. These small raptors know their monkeys; they never associate with the howlers, which lazily browse on flowers and leaves, nor with the fruit-loving spider monkeys. But the insectivorous white-faced capuchin monkeys flush many insects during their noisy, energetic foraging excursions. Leaping from branch to branch, they reach into crevices, tear apart leaf rolls, break open branches, and grab whatever moves. Much of what they scare up, they miss, but the roaches, crickets, and mantids fly out of reach only to be picked off by a diving kite or falcon perching nearby.

The beater species need not be mammalian. The shrike-tanager relies on other bird species in mixed flocks to root among the leaves and bark crevices and to flush out large prey such as katydids, which the shrike then nabs. The most specialized and effective beaters appear to be the swarm-raiding army ants, mainly species of *Eciton* and *Labidus*.

Standing at the leading edge of an army-ant raid is the best way to appreciate what you have been missing in your walk through the forest. Many army ants conduct their raids under-

ground or have relatively small colonies and inconspicuous forays. But some species have worker forces numbering in the hundreds of thousands that stream in diffuse sheets and winding columns through the forest's understory. The workers invade the spaces in the leaf litter, the gaps in root masses, the cracks in bark and tree hollows, exploring all the places into which you wouldn't like to put your hand or face. Some species of insects seem to sense the approach of the raid; social wasps can detect the smell of army ants. If you wear tall rubber boots and smear the tops with citronella or some other repellent, you can stand amid the raid with little fear of the significant bites and stings the ants apply to any biomass they encounter. Here you can see and hear the raw panic of the thousands of normally quiescent, anonymous litter dwellers suddenly roused and exposed. The leading edge of a raid of *Eciton burchelli* is a seething mass of scurrying lizards, spiders, roaches, and beetles. In places, dense swarms of army ants can be seen packed together in a clawing, biting mass from which the jointed tail of a scorpion protrudes. Other species of ants race out of their nests in hollow twigs and fallen logs carrying their broods up and away from the butchery taking place on the forest floor. Crickets and katydids catapult wildly into the air, often with a few army ants clinging to their limbs.

I once watched an *Eciton* raid in which the advance of the ants was clearly marked by a series of strange flies hovering just

Two moths rest on a tree trunk, blending with the color and texture of the bark. They will remain motionless all day, becoming active only at night.

above the ground and shimmering in the patches of sunlight. Their outstretched bodies were bent downward in a right angle, and, periodically, they dropped sharply into the leaf litter and lifted up again. When I netted one, it turned out to be a conopid fly (*Stylogaster*). The bent, probing half of its body was, in fact, an immensely long ovipositor. The flies were diving into the leaf litter and laying eggs on the fleeing insects, which would provide food for the fly larvae should the insects themselves escape an earlier and more rapid dispatch by the ants. The flies were using the ants as beaters.

More conspicuous still are the birds following the raid. Many birds are both facultative and obligate followers of the army ants. An entire family of birds, known sensibly enough as antbirds, follows raids. As many as ten different antbird species may follow a large *Eciton* raid and be joined by a rich array of other birds, such as treecreepers, antshrikes, antwrens, giant ground-cuckoos, ant-tanagers, and—in disturbed habitats—even more casual associates like brown jays and anis. In Mexico, which is beyond the range of many specialized antbirds, as many as twelve species of North American migrants, such as wood thrushes and Kentucky warblers, become army-ant followers. Each species has its own distinctive position in the forest strata and its own foraging technique. Some call noisily, and some flit and hop about rapidly in the understory, behavior that adds to the general impression of frenetic carnage.

The very ecological and taxonomic richness of the phenomenon of beaters and followers suggests the importance of camouflage in rainforests; there must be large numbers of hidden invertebrates to have caused the evolution of such behavior. Birds without beaters must solve the pattern-recognition problem, which means sorting shapes and colors into edible and inedible categories. There is now considerable evidence that birds not only use instinctive cues but also can memorize patterns to develop search images that improve their prey-recognition skills.

Eyes are one of the crucial features shared by prey items that attract a predator's attention, and hiding them is a problem all cryptic animals must solve. Artists have long realized that an eye represented by a simple set of concentric rings of color has a riveting effect on the viewer. This is of more than anthropomorphic significance. Birds often kill their prey with a quick blow to the nerve center. They do this by reacting to and directing their strikes at eyes. Evidently, they pay as much attention to eyes as humans do. Animals that cannot easily conceal their eyes typically mask them by integrating them into a band of color. Frogs, for example, often have a band of dark pigment that is drawn across the body and head, thus obscuring their relatively large eyes.

When predators develop search images and depend on certain recognition cues, it may pay a potential prey species to adopt an unconventional appearance, even if it is at the expense of anonymity. Certain treehoppers have developed bizarre ornaments whose prime function may simply be to prevent the treehopper from being categorized. *Cyphonia*, a genus popularly known as the pawnbroker treehopper, has a dorsal ornament that is an improbable combination of three spikes bearing inflated globular protrusions and spiny processes. These seem far too baroque to

This horned frog (*Proceratophrys* sp.) benefits from its mottled color pattern and bizarre body form in two ways. They make the frog difficult for predators to detect and also enable the frog to act as a sit-and-wait predator of passing insects.

be just a mechanical deterrent, and it is possible that their main function is to obliterate an impression of the conventional homopteran body form. Homopterans such as cicadas, leafhoppers, aphids, and spittlebugs share a similar blunt-headed, smooth, tapering form. Perhaps the ornamented treehoppers are avoiding inclusion in this search image. Such a strategy will work only if the bizarre treehoppers are relatively rare and most birds are searching for more conventionally shaped prey. As a matter of fact, the most bizarre treehoppers are species that never aggregate.

A more typical camouflage strategy is to adopt the pattern of the most common inedible elements of the forest, of which dead leaves are among the most abundant. It is not surprising that many organisms have converged on the same disguise. A brassolid butterfly in flight is often brilliant, yet only the upper surface of its wings is colorful. The underside is mottled grays and browns upon a leaflike network of curving veins. Simply by folding up its wings, the butterfly can settle into the semblance of a leaf to pass the night and those parts of the day that are too cool or too hot for flight.

Katydids are as sophisticated as moths and butterflies in their depiction of all stages of the life and death of leaves. A single species of katydid may have several discrete forms, ranging from individuals that are a healthy, vibrant green to those resembling the final withered, brown, rotting leaf. We look at the notched ends of katydid wings, which are uncanny replicas of insect-damaged leaves, and marvel at how the process of random mutation

stumbles upon such imitations. In many insects, especially those resembling leaf litter and bark, there is often continuous variation so that no two individuals are alike. In this way, the chance that a predator will form a search image for a particular pattern is reduced, and the insect matches the ever-varied nature of the inorganic background.

In Amazonian tributary streams, there is a narrow-bodied fish that exhibits the same extreme modifications and mottled variable color patterns as those of the katydids. The leaffish (*Monocirrhus polyacanthus*) has almost lost the giveaway projecting fins that most fish have. It swims with tiny waves of its transparent anal and dorsal fins, and its tail fin is folded in to resemble a leaf tip. Behaviorally, it adopts a most unfishlike posture—it lies on its side, thereby escaping from both kingfishers and underwater stalkers of small fish. The stem end of the leaf turns out to be a large, triangular-shaped head, most of which is a trapdoor set of jaws. Its harmless appearance allows it to do its own stalking. The leaffish slowly drifts toward small, unsuspecting fish and then seizes them with a sudden gulp.

It is not only small organisms that pattern and posture themselves after tree stubs and leaf litter. *Matamata* turtles in Amazonian ponds and rivers resemble not just a single leaf but a whole mass of rotten, mouldering vegetation that is mimicked by the flanges, folds, and protrusions of their skin. They wait in ambush, ready to dart their long necks out at unwary fish or frogs. In terrestrial situations, potoos are hefty birds that manage to render

The wing covers of katydids, left and right, match both the shape of rainforest leaves and the pattern of venation. They may be green or brown and usually feature blemishes that simulate leaf mold. The sophistication of their disguise is best appreciated when the insect is in its natural environment. The mix of light and shadow and the great variety of leaf shades and hues provide a complex background that is confusing to visual predators.

themselves inconspicuous by virtue of their resemblance to dead tree snags. They are larger versions of the twig moths. All day long, they perch immobile, eyes closed, with their bodies carefully positioned to simulate gray, weathered broken branches. Pauraques, relatives of whip-poor-wills, will nestle on the ground, feet tucked under their bodies, as snug as possible in the leaves, eyes closed and masked by lids that blend with the rest of their earth-toned, streaky plumage.

Camouflage can also be colorful; not all animals that are difficult to see are drab and dull. There are many rainforest birds and insects that shine in shades of emerald, turquoise, gold, and silver. Morpho butterflies, orchid bees, hummingbirds, resplendent quetzals, and the like are responsible for the widespread impression that rainforest insects and birds are more brilliant and spectacular than comparable organisms from other habitats and regions. The coloration of these butterflies and birds seems anything but an effort at concealment. Yet after chasing them with a net or binoculars, one realizes that their optical properties are able to throw off the tracking vertebrate's eye, unable as it is to deal with sharp contrasts in light intensity or to adjust to sudden changes in brightness.

When an eye looks from the sun into the shade, the pupil widens and the retinal field increases. The adaptation to dark reduces the acuity of the observer, and, more important, it increases the observer's reaction time because the brain has to process information from more receptor cells. In addition, the retina is unable to adjust to rapid fluctuations in brightness. A bright image will continue to stimulate the retina after the light ceases or moves. The change in brightness and the darting in and out of sunlight and shade may make it impossible for a predator to pinpoint the prey item accurately in space.

The feathers and exoskeleton of organisms such as hummingbirds and many butterflies are colored brilliantly not by pigments but by the interaction of direct light on a diffracting structure. The feathers and scales refract direct sunlight and reflect iridescent color. A blue morpho is conspicuous as it flits about in sunlight, but in primary rainforest, spots of direct sunlight are small and patchily distributed. As the butterfly passes suddenly from brilliant sunlight to heavy shade, it seems to disappear. Its scaly upper-wing surface owes all its spectacular luster to the reflection and refraction of direct sunlight; in the shade, its tones become somber. So, too, a hummingbird's body will fairly burn with color as it hovers in the sun, but as soon as it passes into the shade, its drab hues blend with the forest background. It is these sudden changes from brilliant to drab that give protection from the pursuits of visual predators.

A bird's color often matches the stratum of the forest it uses. Many birds, such as parrots, hummingbirds, and motmots, look bold and bright in isolation, but they are predominantly emeralds and blues that match the reflectivity of well-lit vegetation. The hermit hummingbirds of the understory and the antbirds, woodcreepers, and ovenbirds of low-light thickets are usual-

ly dark and mottled in browns and grays. Tree frogs are often green, and some have developed the same spectral reflectivity as leaves, while the frogs of the dark-litter zone are frequently brown. Many butterflies, especially ithomiines and satyrids, that habitually frequent the shady understory have transparent wings or combine transparent hind wings with dull brown forewings; there is nothing bright about them. But close relatives that frequent light gaps, sunny areas, and the canopy often possess colorful, light-reflecting pigments.

Larger animals must pattern themselves after a mixture of both sun and shade. Camouflage in this case does not always equate with palatability and harmlessness. The mottled young tapir or fawn may be innocuous and prime fare for many predators, but other cryptically patterned animals—jaguars and anacondas, for example—are not; the purpose of their camouflage is for concealment when hunting.

It is these large camouflaged predators that provide the most psychologically impressive demonstrations of the effectiveness of disruptive colorations. On one of my field trips in Costa Rica, I warned the students about the danger of overlooking such animals when walking along the trails. They did not really believe my warnings; in fact, I did not take them seriously enough myself.

On our first hike, there were plenty of conspicuous distractions—a blue-flowering *Faramea* shrub and some spectacular fig-tree crowns adorned with newly flushed leaves. We sauntered along the trail casually, eyes up, when suddenly the student behind me let loose a gasp and a garbled but unmistakable exclamation of alarm. I stopped dead and looked in the direction of his gesticulating hand. Finally, it dawned upon me that I was a mere yard away from a very large fer-de-lance coiled neatly beside the path.

We backed up and waited for the other students bringing up the rear, who experienced the same problem I had: they had

The pauraque (*Nyctidromus albicollis*), left, is a superb example of protective camouflage. Its brown and buff, streaked and mottled plumage blends perfectly with the leaf litter on the forest floor. By contrast, the camouflage of the bushmaster (*Lachesis stenophrys*), right, is primarily aggressive, allowing it to ambush its prey. The highly venomous bushmaster is the biggest viper in the world, occasionally reaching a length of almost 13 feet (4 m).

to walk to within two yards of it and have it pointed out before they could really see it. That is an unsettling feature of both the fer-de-lance and the much larger and more formidable bushmaster. Both snakes are cryptically patterned, with glossy skin cross-hatched in browns, grays, and tans that render them difficult to detect even at short range. We learned later that half a dozen students ahead of us had passed right by the snake, blissfully oblivious to its presence.

Most of us would be happier if the fer-de-lance had evolved a luminescent lemon skin marked with purple stripes. Such warning coloration would save the snake unwanted encounters that can lead to the waste of its venom and to broken fangs, and it would prevent numerous deaths and mutilations of the many *campesinos* who step on or pass too close to this relatively pugnacious viper. Instead, the pattern of a fer-de-lance is the evolutionary triumph of crypsis over advertisement. Along with bushmasters, boas, pythons, anacondas, and many rattlers, the fer-de-lance has a camouflage pattern. These big reptiles are all ambush-style predators: they sit and wait for their prey to blunder within striking range. Food is far more important to them than warning away potential predators and wandering heavy-footed mammals.

There is a kind of horror that comes with this discovery about the big snakes, but few naturalists will forgo a chance to see one of the legendary serpents in the field. Typically, someone tells you there is a fer-de-lance or bushmaster right over there at the base

of the tree. You go over carefully, excited about getting your first look at one of the most dangerous snakes in the Americas. You inch ahead, aware that a fer-de-lance is willing to strike when threatened and that the inch-long (2 cm) fangs can deliver a voluminous gush of tissue-destroying toxins. Your eyes search the leaf litter closely but see no snake. You lean closer, head extended and everything else held back; you stare yet see nothing. You advance a little more, and still more, until suddenly and awfully it materializes, a huge puddle of snake coiled right before your eyes.

By then, you are close enough to see all the details that formerly were just part of the blur of light and shade, old leaves and twigs. Up close, you see the luster of the skin that gives it its Costa Rican name "velvet." You see the hard, impersonal yellow eyes, the malevolent eyebrow ridges, and the huge wedge-shaped head swelling at the base. Can those be the venom glands? The large pits in the nasal area of the face, its infrared heat-sensing organs, are remarkably deep. You wonder how you missed it before, yet when you stand back, the monster virtually dissolves into the forest floor. With a sinking feeling, you realize just how many more you have missed in the past and how many you will miss again.

At such moments, the words of British zoologist Hugh Cott, preeminent student of adaptive coloration, come to mind. When we are lucky enough to see the hidden and their artistry is revealed, especially in this form, we had best "look on in wonder and in gratitude."

Osa
Where wilderness remains

On the seaward side of Corcovado National Park, lush forested hillsides drop precipitously into the Pacific Ocean. The Corcovado coast is a rare place where tracks of jaguars and tapirs can be seen side-by-side on the beach.

The mouth of the Sirena River is an excellent place to watch for wildlife. It is a regular crossing place for Baird's tapirs, while American crocodiles (*Crocodylus acutus*) and sharks are often seen in the surf where the river meets the ocean.

Tuna schools ahead, spider monkey troops behind. Jutting out into the Pacific in southern Costa Rica, the Osa Peninsula is a unique place where one can watch both of these increasingly rare animals without shifting place. In most of the wet tropics the coastline has been thoroughly deforested and heavily settled. The Osa is a happy exception. Lack of road access prevented much agricultural settlement until the 1960s. The 1970s saw the creation of the magnificent Corcovado National Park in the cen-

tral Pacific coastal region of the Osa and the establishment of the Golfo Dulce Forest Reserve along the hilly curving spine of the peninsula. This limited the extent to which large-scale plantation agriculture and large logging operations were able to alter the Osa. As a result there are long stretches of coast where a high wall of primary rainforest stands flush against the open sea.

At the head of the dark sand beach, you may sit looking out over the limitless monochrome expanse of bright sky and Pacific horizon, while immediately behind you, the forest looms complex and cacophonous, woven and dark. Between the crashing of breakers, the rising electric shrill of cicadas blends with the sucking sound of the retreating, foaming surf. A coatimundi digs for sea turtle eggs and a black hawk perched on a leaning coco palm eyes a purple and orange *Geocarcinus* crab preoccupied with a meal of fallen fruit. This juxtaposition of forest and sea produces some unusual ecological relationships. The Osa is one of those rare places where sea turtle is part of the diet of jaguars.

At the mouths of the rivers one can see tapir grazing placidly on the beach hibiscus. Nearby, on a turning tide, bull sharks cruise in hunt of the abundant snapper and snook. I was once chased up a tree by a snorting, teeth-clacking clan of white-lipped peccary along the Sirena River, which drains the southern section of Corcovado National Park. If there is something approximating wilderness left in Costa Rica it is on the Osa.

As a peninsula extending into the Pacific, the Osa is naturally buffered against rapid climate change by the influence of ocean currents and local cloud formation. Much of the area gets 200 inches (5,000 mm) of rain a year. It is like a small outlier of Amazonian forest. A number of Amazonian trees find their most northerly limit on the Osa but are absent on the Central American mainland.

Predictable moisture may be what allows the Osa to act like a pocket of Amazonia. The constant availability of ocean-derived rainfall keeps the Osa humid even during the dry season. This oceanic influence may explain why the Osa is both extremely diverse and characterized by high endemism. The region hosts 3,100 species of plants (including 750 tree species), of which 67 are endemic to the Osa. Vertebrates show equally high endemicity. For example, of the forty species of freshwater fish found in the area, nine are endemic to the Osa. There are three types of endemic birds. Perhaps these endemics evolved and persisted here through periods of great historical climate change because the Osa is buffered just like a very humid oceanic island.

As much as the Osa's diversity and endemism, it is the juxtaposition of the sea and the forest that is so appealing and that adds immeasurably to the richness of the natural history. The huge mangroves in the north of the Osa, at the mouth of the Sierpe River, are the biggest and most well preserved on the Pacific coast of Mesoamerica. This is one of the few places on Earth where one can see a mangrove hummingbird or pale-billed cotinga. Lurking in the tangle of roots are 13-foot-long (4 m) American crocodiles and huge black snook up to 5 feet (1.5 m) long. The beaches in the area are still relatively free of light pollution. This year Friends of the Osa, a conservation group active in the area, documented more than two thousand five hundred olive ridley sea turtle nestings on just a few miles of beach. Recent studies have shown that having forest along the nesting areas on the beach is favorable to sea turtles, because the shade moderates the temperature of the sand. Sea turtles, like many reptiles, have a curious means of determining gender. The temperature at which an egg is incubated determines if the embryo will develop into a male or female. If the forest is removed, the uniformly high sand temperatures will produce mainly females and lower the viability of the turtle population.

Large scale deforestation in the Osa is confined to the flatter lowlands. The hilly areas—and most of the Osa is hilly—are usually heavily forested. This is true even on areas outside of the national parks. This private forest is entirely necessary for the parks that exist on the Osa (i.e., Corcovado and Piedras Blancas National Parks). These are beautifully blanketed in forest, but they are far too small to maintain adequate populations of big predators such as jaguars and harpy eagles, or wide-ranging species such as scarlet macaws and white-lipped peccary. Virtually all the national parks in Central America and North America are too small to be ecologically viable in the long term. They were created before people understood how much space jaguars, macaws, and peccaries need, and after much of the forest had been converted to agriculture. Fortunately, on the Osa the two national parks, Corcovado to the west and Piedras Blancas to the east, are still surrounded and connected by a patchwork of primary and secondary forest.

Much of the forest outside the parks is quasi-protected, either because it lies within private reserves created by landowners or because it is owned by eco-lodges whose owners know the forest is their bread and butter. The economy of the Osa has shifted away from subsistence agriculture to a service economy driven by sportfishing and ecotourism. This has reduced the role of hunting in local culture. Although poaching of wildife still occurs, it is not for subsistence food consumption. It is now just an illegal form of recreation that is steadily coming under control. As a result, the wildlife is not confined to just the national parks. Too often the wildlife of parks is marooned by the hostile surrounding landscape. But on the Osa the wildlife still makes use of the broader landscape.

My wife Sharon and I own a patch of the forest on the Osa. It is a full hour's drive from the nearest boundary of Corcovado. But while staying there I feel as though I am living in a national park. When the *Calophyllum* trees are dropping their bluish gray marble-like fruits, I have counted, while sitting by my house, as many as twenty guans foraging on them. These large, meaty—and reputedly delicious—birds attract both jaguars and pumas within sight of the house. A large male tapir has been walking about the garden of late and there is a daily parade of spider, white-faced capuchin, and howler monkeys. A pair of noisy scarlet macaws nests in a large *Carapa* tree-limb cavity in full view of my hammock. This is not atypical. On the Osa most private property, except for the large coastal cattle ranches and rice farms, is wildlife friendly. This mix of private and public lands is why the Osa still supports jaguars and macaws. As a result, the Osa stands as one of the best places to see neotropical wildlife. I know of no better place to gain an introduction to wet tropical forest.

Others agree. Tourism is rising steadily on the Osa. The attractiveness and accessibility of the Osa for tourism can be either its salvation or damnation. Managed low-volume, high-quality tourism could be compatible with healthy wildlife populations and it could be the core of the local economy. But large marinas, fish farms, and international airports are planned by people who live far from the Osa's forests, its rivers, and its bays. Such developments will degrade the very reason one might want to visit the Osa. Right now the balance between wildlife and development is healthy. The forest is frayed around the edges, but the hallmarks of ecological wilderness persist. There is still time for Costa Rica to give wilderness its due place in the Osa.

Corcovado National Park is the most pristine expanse of lowland forest in Costa Rica—a wilderness that provides sanctuary for some of Costa Rica's most exciting and impressive wildlife, including the Baird's tapir, above, scarlet macaw, right, and jaguar, far right.

The southern Pacific rainforests, including those of the Osa Peninsula, have long been isolated from the rest of Costa Rica by drier forests to the north and south and by the Talamanca mountains to the east. As a result of isolation, the area has long been a center for speciation. Birds confined to the southern Pacific forests include the orange-collared manakin, top left, and fiery-billed araçari, bottom left. The black-cheeked ant-tanager, right, has a more restricted range, being endemic to the Osa Peninsula and the adjoining Golfo Dulce lowlands.

The mangrove forests around the Osa Peninsula, top left, are among the richest and most extensive in Costa Rica. They provide a refuge for numerous rare species, including the American crocodile (*Crocodylus acutus*), bottom left. A number of birds are confined to mangroves, including the mangrove warbler (*Dendroica petechia erithachorides*), above, and the endangered mangrove hummingbird (*Amazilia boucardi*), right, which is endemic to the Pacific coast of Costa Rica.

Reptiles and amphibians that are characteristic of the Osa Peninsula include the black-headed bushmaster (*Lachesis melanocephala*), left, and two poison dart frogs—the granular poison dart frog (*Dendrobates granuliferus*), top right, and Golfo Dulcean poison dart frog (*Phyllobates vittatus*), bottom right.

The virtues of sloth
Adaptation to life in the canopy

We owe a debt to the sloth: according to the Tucuna Indians who live along the Brazil-Colombia border, it was the sloth that let light into the world. As they explain, "In the beginning, the Earth lay in darkness. All was cloaked in the deep shade of a giant *Ceiba* tree. The night monkey, unconstrained by darkness, daily climbed and fed on *Parkia* tree fruits. Each day when he relieved himself and looked up, he could see a glow above. By throwing the spent *Parkia* fruit hulls upward, he gradually knocked a thousand openings in the darkness overhead that allowed some light to break through. Stars were thus born. In search of more light, the night monkey and a brother enlisted the help of termites and ants to cut the trunk of the great *Ceiba*. The deed was done, but even then, the tree remained mysteriously upright, suspended, as it were, from the celestial vault above. They enlisted the help of a squirrel, who after some investigation found a sloth up above using his strong grip to hold the tree upright. The squirrel blinded the sloth by throwing a handful of ants in its eyes, whereupon the sloth let go of the tree. The giant crashed to the Earth. And there was light."

The use of the sloth as a cosmological symbol is widespread throughout South American rainforest cultures, a reflection of the sloth's abundance in the forests' leafy summits. It is also an indication of the aboriginal skill in animal observation, a visual skill not

Although they are slow-moving, brown-throated three-toed sloths are highly acrobatic. They climb, dangle, and maneuver with the great agility afforded by their flexible joints and long, powerful limbs. Sloths travel through the canopy along a network of horizontal branches and vines, moving limb over limb, suspended by their hooklike claws.

to be underestimated. I know many tropical biologists who have never seen a sloth in the field. All five species are difficult to spot. When they are at rest—and they rest much of their lives—only the keenest eyes can pick them out. In Panama, sloths may be as thick as eight per 2.5 acres (1 hectare), an astonishing number for a rather hefty rainforest mammal. But to most people, they remain hidden, not so much by the density of foliage, backlit by the powerful equatorial sky, but by their slow, sleepy nature.

Three-toed, the best-known species, are most easily spotted from a river, a vantage point that permits a view of the tree crowns under good light conditions and that perhaps accounts for the once popular myth that sloths feed only on *Cecropia* trees. Cecropias are abundant pioneer colonists of riverbanks and light gaps, and they have an open architecture. Although their leaves are favored by sloths, both the three-toed and the two-toed species will eat a wide variety of tree leaves and usually only leaves. Among the most specialized folivores in the world, sloths are adapted to exploit the concentration of foliage in the upper reaches of tropical forest.

The ancestor of the three-toed sloth, and of the other edentate (toothless) mammals, such as armadillos and anteaters, was almost certainly an insectivore, a heritage that has left the sloth at something of a disadvantage for life as a herbivore. Its zygomatic arches, which contain and anchor the jaw's chewing muscles, are incompletely filled. Nevertheless, sloths rank as one of the most highly adapted folivores. They are superbly engineered for a lifetime of suspension, hanging upside down high above the forest floor.

The adaptive elegance of sloths has only recently been fully appreciated. In the past, sloths have been seen as an almost catatonic accident of nature. Comte de Buffon, the famous eighteenth-century French biologist-savant, bought a pet two-toed

Much of the life of the brown-throated three-toed sloth is spent sleeping high in the canopy in rain or sun. Its bulky, fibrous diet of leaves requires long periods of time for digestion.

sloth from a schooner in Amsterdam and, after much examination, pronounced it a horrid misfit. Buffon's analysis of the sloth's habits and morphology led him to explain that "the inertia of this animal is not so much due to laziness as to wretchedness; it is the consequence of its faulty structure. Inactivity, stupidity, and even habitual suffering result from its strange and ill-constructed conformation." His condemnation goes on, and he concludes that "everything about it shows its wretchedness and proclaims it to be one of those defective monsters, those imperfect sketches, which nature has sometimes formed and which, having scarcely the faculty of existence, could only continue for a short time and have since been removed from the catalogue of living beings. They are the last possible term among creatures of flesh and blood, and any further defect would have made their existence impossible." Such is the view of a great scientist who, for all his established mental acuity and knowledge, unfortunately lived before the concept of natural selection.

Buffon, who never saw a sloth in its arboreal haunts, may have been puzzled by the difficulty sloths have in getting around a conventional animal cage or human domicile. An old natural history book I have, a work compiled in 1823, contains an illustration of a sloth that was no doubt drawn by a British artist working from a stuffed museum specimen. It shows the sloth standing erect in a curious quadruped posture, with its long forelegs and shorter hind legs forcing it into a sprinter's stance. Its long claws curve along the ground. However, as naturalist Charles Waterton pointed out, such a posture would have been unachievable, for "the sloth has no heels." In reality, a sloth on the ground is a gruesomely awkward sight. Because it is literally incapable of standing upright, its belly scrapes against the earth. Its limbs sprawl and splay fore and aft, and it can move only by reaching ahead, wrapping its claws around some fixed object or digging them into the soil and dragging its body across the ground. In this position, the sloth is not only ludicrous but—more important—defenseless. One can imagine why Buffon, who observed the sloth in this state, summed it up as "the picture of innate misery."

A sloth must hang; it is at its best when suspended upside down from a horizontal limb. In that position, it can do all it needs to do—feed, sleep, breed, walk, and whistle. Waterton, who traveled in the Guianas, was one of the first naturalists to see sloths in the field. He countered Buffon's assessment by pointing out that "this singular animal is destined by nature to live and die in the trees; and to do justice to him, naturalists must examine him in his upper element." That perspective should be brought to our consideration of all organisms: we are blind to the virtues and splendor of an organism if we do not see it in the place where it evolved.

The sloth's most conspicuous adaptation to the upper echelons of rainforest is its feet. Essentially large hooks, they have been reduced in complexity and width, drawn out and tipped with long claws able to curve around small limbs. The last joints of the digits do the holding. A much more effective way to grasp a tubular surface than with a fist, the sloth's hooklike grip remains strong even when the wrist is being twisted and rotated. The sloth's limb joints are very loosely encapsulated, and the articulating bones have rounded surfaces without the channels and

flanges that constrain and strengthen most joints, allowing for acrobatic maneuvering. In fact, the sloth's feet can rotate almost 180 degrees. Try this with your own feet; even ballet dancers can manage only 90 degrees. The sloth is thus able to move with slow but superb agility along the branching array of lianas and tree limbs that constitute its highways.

The consequence of the sloth's special foot structure is a dependence on thin supports; it cannot manage well on a hefty horizontal branch. Apparently limited to localities with plenty of lianas, sloths are, however, good swimmers and make reasonable headway with a long-limbed dog paddle. (This serves them in good stead in riverbank and floodplain habitats, which, although often liana-poor, support relatively nutritious types of vegetation, including *Cecropia* trees. Even the sloth sometimes falls off a limb into the water.)

The oldest natural history book in my collection was written by someone ignorant of the fact that sloths are able to move smoothly through the canopy on their network of lianas and

Brown-throated three-toed sloths are often observed in *Cecropia* trees, whose leaves are a common food of theirs. The open, sunny architecture of this tree makes the sloths relatively easy to see.

limbs. The author concocted the following rather ingenious theory of movement: "The sloth subsists entirely on vegetable food, and as it requires a considerable share of provision, it generally strips a tree of all its verdure in less than a fortnight. It then falls to devouring the bark and thus in a short time destroys the very source of its support. When this is the case, being unable to descend, it is obliged to drop from the branches to the ground; and after remaining some time torpid, from the violence of its fall, it prepares for a tedious, dangerous, and painful migration to some neighboring tree."

That creative scenario may have been stimulated by the fact that sloths do seem to be almost moribund at times. Even when

Hoffmann's two-toed sloths are more aggressive in defense than their three-toed relatives. Their ferocious threat display shows off their formidable claws and teeth to best advantage.

fully awake, they move so slowly that it can be almost painful to watch. This apparent laziness gives the sloth its popular name in both Spanish and English and is explained by the Bororo tribes with the following myth:

"Long ago, the sloth was not easygoing. He moved rapidly through the forest and had a nasty, greedy temperament. One day, the Almighty decided to descend to Earth. He waited four weeks until the hole in the sky known as the moon was fully open, and then He climbed down on a liana. On His arrival, He went to drink at a water hole. A group of animals—a tapir, a hare, a jaguar, an anteater, and others—all stepped aside so that He could drink first. All but the sloth. The sloth pushed ahead and drank greedily and at great length. This, of course, angered the Almighty One, and He announced to the sloth that in punishment, He would cast a spell. The terrified sloth expected death. But the Almighty just breathed on him, snuffing out forever his greed and thirst. With great relief, the sloth smiled, and since then, he has never had another drink and has been as easygoing as they get."

If we doubt this account, we need not accept instead Buffon's claim that the sloth's idleness is a consequence of wretched design. It is more accurately described as superb energy conservation. The sloth's metabolism is as specialized as its morphology and reflects the requirements of life as an arboreal leaf eater.

The three-toed sloth's low-energy diet is made up of large volumes of leaves whose many calories are bound up in hard-to-digest cellulose. A huge, multichambered stomach that functions much like the digestive system of cows and other ruminants fills one-third of the sloth's body and is rich in bacteria capable of digesting cellulose. The leaves may spend as long as a month in the stomach before moving on to the small intestine. But a high-fiber diet digested on this small scale apparently does not produce the calories necessary to sustain the elevated body temperatures typical of mammals. Instead, the sloth's body temperature fluctuates, rising in daytime as it forages and declining at night or when it is sleeping and digestion is taking place.

At the best of times, however, the sloth's body temperature is low, ranging from 86 to 93 degrees F (30 to 34 degrees C)—well below the 98.6 degrees F (37 degrees C) typical of humans and the even higher temperatures of smaller mammals. At night, it may drop close to ambient temperatures in the range of 70+ degrees F (20+ degrees C). Body size seems to affect the distribution and activity patterns of the two major types of sloths. The larger two-toed sloths occupy tropical mountain slopes and range into the cloud forest, while the three-toed sloths remain confined to lower elevations. Perhaps because of their greater energy requirements, the three-toed sloths are more active both day and night than are their two-toed relatives.

When at rest, a sloth does its best to pull itself into a compact, hanging-basket shape by moving its long, heat-radiating feet toward each other on the limb. In a tree crotch, it assumes a com-

Brown-throated three-toed sloths are good swimmers and are sometimes encountered crossing rivers or lakes.

pletely spherical posture, burying its nearly naked clown face in its chest fur. Its long, shaggy fur coat looks more appropriate for an Arctic mammal than for a denizen of the sweltering, humid tropics, but in fact, the hairiness of the sloth is in part an adaptation to conserve heat. Special grooves on each hair support blue-green algae that undergo population explosions according to the regime of rainfall. During the dry season, sloths turn gray and brown, growing darker and greener when the rains come. This mossy, coarse pelage gives them a cryptic, poorly defined shape when they hang immobile overhead. The Machiguenga Indians of the eastern Peruvian lowlands, who, like all tribes, have their own names for the constellations of stars, thus apply their word for sloth to the amorphous twin galaxies, the Magellanic Clouds. (The Brazilian Mundurucú have seized on a shorter-range image of the sloth. When seen from a few yards away, a sloth looks much like a hanging weaving. The Mundurucú therefore credit the sloth with the invention of the hammock, which veterans of languid tropical afternoons acknowledge as one of the finest discoveries known to civilization.)

All of these features allow the well-insulated, slow-burning sloth to make do with only half the normal metabolic rate of other comparably sized mammals. But there is a cost to such thermal conservation: the need to reactivate on cool mornings. A sloth does not have a large muscle mass capable of generating much heat through shivering, nor does it have the mass to retain heat once it is generated. Instead, it raises its temperature by

sunbathing. At dawn, the sloth will dangle from the peak of the eastern face of a tree crown, basking more like some strangely hairy, tailless reptile than a warm-blooded mammal. Sunbathing literally warms its blood.

This is also the time that the three-toed sloth exposes a brilliant orange-red patch of fine fur along its back. This single flamboyant act has earned it the aboriginal name "sun sloth" in some areas, and while the skin flag's social significance is unknown, either mate attraction or territorial advertisement are possibilities. Although the three-toed sloth will now and then whistle in monotones, other aspects of its social life seem remarkably dull; copulation appears to be a rare event. And there is only one report, an eyewitness account by herpetologist Harry Greene, of two sloths fighting, apparently for possession of a Cecropia tree.

The sloth's seemingly minimal use of visual signals may account for its strikingly rigid facial expressions. In keeping with the economy of the sloth, which has one of the lowest muscle weights of all mammals relative to its size and limb lengths, its facial musculature is greatly reduced except for the chewing apparatus. The fixed, almost smiling expression is particularly noticeable in the three-toed sloth and is perhaps coupled with the low intelligence quotient that most folivores appear to possess. A recent natural history text notes that the sloth's "sadly vacuous expression gives the impression that it entertains an actual thought on alternate Tuesdays."

There may be a good ecological reason for such undemonstrative behavior. Social signals such as whistling or exposing its orange back flag—even sunbathing or just plain movement—make the sloth vulnerable to predation because of its slow speed. Although human hunters complain that sloths seem to be composed mainly of hair, bone, and stringy sinews, many animals, given the opportunity, will eat sloths; friends of mine have seen them killed by tayra weasels and pumas.

Sloths are not completely defenseless. Their limbs have a slow but amazing strength, not unlike that of a pneumatic piston moving inexorably in its designated direction. If a sloth wants to drag its great hooked nails across your body, you had better move out of the way. The two-toed sloth is especially pugnacious compared with the three-toed, and it will advertise the menace of its claws by hanging from its hind feet with its forelimbs spread, showing its prominent hooked toes, mouth agape, and expelling air. It is a ritualized display with a convincing message. It is also a good chance to see how incredibly stained the sloth's large side teeth are by its diet of tannin- and alkaloid-laced leaves; the teeth are the same hue as those of one of my tobacco-chewing neighbors.

After it is detected, the sloth's best defense is distance. A sloth, whether threatened or resting, can usually dangle from thin lianas that are inaccessible to most arboreal cats and weasels. But the keen-eyed harpy eagle, the world's heaviest eagle, with wrists as thick as your own and talons as long as a grizzly's claws, is able to snag the sloth, yank it from its holdfast and use the lifting power of its huge, broad wings to carry it off. Several different (and highly courageous) studies of harpy nests have found that the sloth constitutes the single largest component of the harpy's diet, followed by monkeys, porcupines, opossums, and other mammals.

The presence of a harpy or other predator must have a considerable impact on sloth populations. I suspect such predation was common until the recent extirpation of large predators in areas such as Barro Colorado Island in Panama and much of Costa Rica. That may be one reason sloths show little evidence of territoriality. Considerable overlap in the home range of sloths occurs without any overt hostility when they are close together. Along a river canal in northeastern Costa Rica, I saw three adult three-toed sloths all within sight of each other. Natural predation rates in areas that still retain harpy eagles, cats, and other predators, coupled with the sloth's slow metabolism, may keep populations below the carrying capacity of the vegetation. In addition, the reproductive rate of sloths is low; after the two-toed sloth's 304-day pregnancy, a single offspring is born, and there is a long interval between successive births.

A lean diet combined with arboreality probably explains the low birth weight of sloths. One of the rare measurements of a newborn three-toed sloth revealed that its weight was only 5 percent that of an adult. In mammalian terms, that is a low figure (especially considering that only a single offspring is born) and one that is on a par with human birth weights. And also like humans, the sloth offspring are slow to mature. The infant three-toed sloth clings to its mother for a full six months before becoming independent.

Like all adaptations, those of the sloth cannot be fully appraised in taxonomic isolation any more than they could be appraised in Buffon's cage. The special adaptive pinnacle the sloth occupies is best understood by comparing it with the other mammals of the tropical-forest canopy. The sloth shares some adaptations with the related anteaters, which also have a low-energy existence, move phlegmatically, and have fluctuating body temperatures. The anteater with the greatest thermoregulatory problem is the tiny silky anteater, which weighs less than 10 ounces (only a few hundred grams) and is active at night. By day, it hides and, when disturbed, seems incapable of running away. Primatologists in Manú, Peru, have seen big *Cebus* (capuchin) monkeys reach into dense vine clumps, extract one of the beautiful golden creatures, and unhurriedly gnaw down the slowly squirming animal in one of the most appalling demonstrations of nature red in tooth and claw. There is much that is similar about the metabolic and arboreal life histories of these animals. Although the similarity may be a consequence of their shared ancestry, I suspect that is not the case, since such adaptations are not limited to edentate mammals.

Truly convergent life-history patterns are displayed by unrelated arboreal folivores such as hoatzins, iguanas, and howler monkeys. The foliage-feeding hoatzin, a bird that lives along the thickly forested banks of South American lakes and rivers, fits the pattern of inactivity and large size associated with leaf eating. (Flight is not a talent of this bird. It seems barely able to become airborne before its heavy, awkward flapping sends it crashing into the vegetation.) The hoatzin's huge distensible crop constitutes about one-third of its body; empty, it makes up 17.7 percent of the body weight. A true fermentation chamber, the crop is crammed with leaves, especially leguminous vine tips, until the hoatzin achieves a ridiculously heavy front end and a nasty odor. The foregut fermentation is a trait shared with sloths, monkeys, and ruminants but with no other birds; it also accounts for the hoatzin's popular name, "stink bird" (as it smells like cow dung). So, too, the leaf-eating iguanas outweigh all their neotropical rainforest relatives by a wide margin. Ornamented with crests and drooping dewlaps, they spend much of their day in sunny indolence on a tree limb—the classic lounge lizards.

The leaf-eating primates also tend to be like sloths in many respects: both are big, pot-bellied, and prone to snoozing much of their lives away. Time-budget studies show that howlers spend about two-thirds of the day and all of the long tropical night sleeping or otherwise lolling about. They have the remarkable ability to relax enough on a bare limb to fall asleep, a feat they achieve by draping all four legs over the sides and leaving the prehensile tail alongside as a stabilizer. When they move, it is usually to make a short foray in search of the nearest edible flowers, foliage, or fruit. This seeming indolence is in marked contrast to higher-energy monkeys, like the fruit-specialist spider monkeys

The female brown-throated three-toed sloth carries her single offspring with her for several months until the young sloth can forage on its own. The infant clings to its mother's fur and is taken everywhere with her, snuggled up in its own portable hammock from which it views the world with lively curiosity.

Hoatzins, which live along lake and river margins in the South American rainforest, share at least one trait with sloths: both animals are leaf-eaters. These birds have a huge crop that they pack with leaves for fermentative digestion.

that race through the treetops, brachiating with long, rapid arm swings and leaping energetically across the treetop chasms. Similarly, the insectivorous squirrel monkeys seem to be perpetually on the move, never pausing to rest.

Of all the above arboreal folivores, it is monkeys like the howlers that are taxonomically closest to sloths. But Claude Levi-Strauss, the French anthropological structuralist, finds great contrast in the cultural interpretation of the two animals. According to his rather rigid system of dichotomy, Indians use sloths as models of cleanliness and howlers as models of filth, a distinction that parallels the differences in metabolic rate of the two animals. Sloths defecate but once a week and, for some still unknown reason, laboriously descend to the ground to deposit their droppings in a depression they scrape at the base of the tree with their tail stub. The sloth gut-passage time spans days and weeks compared with about twenty hours for howlers and a mere four hours for spider monkeys.

Contrary to the sloth's careful, surreptitious disposal, howlers have a bombs-away attitude to this event, and they are not averse to anointing naturalists and other interlopers with their copious and pungent waste products. They are often quite good at targeting, and the combination of height and gravity gives their messages an impact that cannot be ignored. Primatologist Frank Carpenter saw the howlers' careful effort at marksmanship as a sign of intelligence, remarking that "an individual would slowly

approach to a place directly above me, or as nearly as possible, and then would release excrement . . . . Seemingly, the dropping of branches and excrement is a kind of primitive instrumental act." In other words, the act of dung-mediated dissuasion is much like tool use. In any case, these observations reflect large differences between the digestive and feeding rates of the sloth and the howler. But there are also similarities.

Howlers let go with a major evacuation promptly upon waking at dawn. One might reliably place the splattering noise and the vocal roaring that accompanies it in the sort of daytime clock of natural noises that used to be constructed in Europe from the predictable sequence of birdsongs. What this means mechanically and physiologically is that howlers empty themselves like clockwork and so create new space for the next mass of fodder. For both sloths and howlers, the timing is probably a more stringent procedure than it would be for an omnivore or a carnivore. Both have to feed on a regular, uninterrupted basis; otherwise, they would quickly starve.

The scatological convergence between howlers and sloths goes further. Both have a rich array of coprophagous (dung-eating) arthropodal affiliations. A sloth population in Brazil was found to have no fewer than nine species of coprophagous moths and beetles associated with its dung—nine unique, dependent kinds of creatures. Howler dung has a less specialized, more diverse set of followers and

Sloth hair is unlike that of any other mammal. It is coarse and grooved and is often colored green, especially during the rainy season. The green color is due to microscopic single-celled, green algae that grow on the surface of the hair. Sloth hair is populated by sloth moths (Pyralidae), which lay their eggs on sloth dung when their host descends to the ground to defecate.

feeders. At Barro Colorado Island, Panama, more than two dozen species of scarab beetles breed using howler dung, as do many flies and other types of beetles. Some of these beetles no doubt have catholic tastes as far as the taxonomy of their benefactors is concerned. However, I have found that in areas where all other species of monkeys and most herbivorous mammals have been eliminated, the presence of howlers is enough to sustain a vigorous population of scarabs, many of which are unexpectedly beautiful, ornamented with horns and bodies that shimmer with iridescent copper, blue, and green. They are appreciated by birds such as motmots, themselves a spectacle of blue-green elegance. The motmots carry the largest scarabs up to a perch and tenderize them by repeated smacks on the limb before swallowing. The digestive process of these leaf eaters thus connects leaves, beetles, and birds.

Significantly more attractive than the dung of carnivores like cats or raptors, which offers up only dry pellets of hair and bone fragments, herbivore dung is rich in nutrients. Many of the toxic secondary compounds in the leaves have been metabolized, and the dung is often loaded with bacterially derived vitamins such as the B-complex series. All in all, the dung of sloths and monkeys seems to be a good thing to eat for those animals that have no evolutionary reason to be proud or fastidious, and there is an abundant enough source for large numbers of beetles to have specialized in it.

Both the sloth and the howler crop a measurable proportion of the rainforest's total tree-leaf production; sloths remove something like 2 percent, and howlers may consume somewhat more. Coupled with the array of moths and beetles that feeds on their dung, these leaf eaters may be an important loop in the movement of nutrients through the food chain. They help make possible the continuous, almost frenetic flow of nutrients that is a rainforest. They may rest often, but as they rest, they digest, and in their capacious gut sac of foliage, they prepare the means of existence for a network of other dependent organisms, transferring the gains of one set of tree species into forms available to others. This important role is made possible only by the low-energy physiology of the special mammals that patiently pass their days feeding a little and sleeping a great deal, draped indolently throughout the upper reaches of the forest.

As Waterton long ago advised, the sloth's languorous approach to life is best appreciated when it is considered in its natural habitat, in the land of the midday siesta. The sloth exemplifies the rightness of that combination of hammock, the arrival of the afternoon rains typical of rainforests, and the noonday bout of herbivory—say, a heavy plate of rice and field yucca. As we close our eyes and drop away into our own episode of digestive slumber, the ecological rationale of such behavior becomes evident, and we can fully savor the virtues of sloth.

Beetlejuice
Chemical defense by insects & other arthropods

My friend and sometime field assistant Dave Bell is a trusting soul. In planning a trip to Monteverde, Costa Rica, his first to the tropics, he had naturally expressed a concern about biohazards like venomous snakes and insects. When I told him that his destination was one of the safest, most benign habitats on Earth, he believed me.

"No worry, it's cool cloud forest," I nonchalantly explained. "Compared with lowland rainforest or even with the Ontario bush, it's tame."

Montane rainforest and especially cloud forest is, in fact, an easy place to work. Snake diversity drops off sharply with altitude, and populations of the biggest and most aggressive vipers, such as bushmasters, the fer-de-lance, and the large cascabel rattlesnakes, dwindle as one passes into the cool, cloud-draped regions of mossy forest. Less lethal but still significant hazards such as ants, stinging and otherwise, are ubiquitous in the lowlands, but true cloud forest has few ants and is almost free of the large ponerine ants, a group that administers a fiery injection. Both the big snakes and ants need warmer temperatures and more sun than a place like Monteverde offers. I could think of hardly anything toxic enough for my friend to worry about. It was my honest opinion that the cloud forest was almost hazard-free. As Dave discovered, I was quite mistaken.

The very first night that Dave spent in Monteverde, he went "black lighting." Entomologists often set up an ultraviolet light in front of a white sheet at night, using the glowing ultraviolet radiation to attract moths and other night-flying insects. Dave had arrived at the prime time for this activity. It was the start of wet season, when dormant moths break out of their chrysalises, crawl from the soil, forsake their protective crevices, and begin to fly in search of food, mates, and reproductive frontiers.

The collecting sheet and light were well placed on a hotel balcony overlooking a forested ravine. Soon after the light was lit, insects swarmed in out of the night. Huge green katydids, copper-colored scarab beetles, large and elegantly patterned hawkmoths, and clouds of smaller fry swirled about the light, landing on the sheet and on the clothes of Dave and a few fellow entomologists. Among the insects were hundreds of beautiful, yet tiny, rove beetles arrayed in attractive orange and metallic gunmetal blue. The beetles were thick, but the entomologists were not concerned. With a killing jar in one hand, a cold beer in the other, and a face full of insects, an entomologist could only be happy.

Dave's first experience of the tropics' exotic fauna met all his expectations, and he went to bed satisfied. But in the morning, he awoke feeling as though he were hung over. He was tired, nauseated, and dizzy; his neck burned painfully, and after turning red, it broke out in large blisters that looked like second-degree burns. The sores got steadily worse, oozing lymph and finally bursting into an ugly mass of raw, tortured epidermis. After a few days, half of the skin on his neck was eaten away, and he was unable to turn his head. Pieces of skin the size of quarters flaked off, and Dave grew understandably nervous about his fate. The nightmare I had assured him did not exist in Monteverde was growing on Dave's neck.

Dave's worries ceased only when he learned that he was not, in fact, infected with a microbe or fungus but was under a chemical attack. There is something comforting in knowing that it is not a living, multiplying organism that is destroying your tissue but an

Red bugs (Pyrrhocoridae) typically congregate in large numbers, providing a conspicuous visual warning to predators that they are distasteful.

When molested, the blister beetle (*Cissites maculata*) exudes cantharidin, a caustic secretion that causes severe blistering. If ingested it is potentially fatal.

inanimate compound. The chemical turned out to be formidable, however—it was more potent than cobra venom. The compound destroying Dave's neck was pederin, the most complex nonprotein insect secretion known. Pederin also ranks among the most poisonous of all animal products, more toxic than even recluse spider venom, which is itself some fifteen times more powerful than cobra venom.

The tiny, colorful rove beetles release pederin when crushed. At some point, Dave must have squashed a beetle on his skin. If he had known about this beetle's toxicity, he could have washed off the chemical. But the amounts of toxin were extremely minute, and the beetles themselves seemed innocuous. Undetected, the pederin began to destroy Dave's skin, killing cell after cell as it diffused and worked its way deeper and deeper. The destruction stopped only when the pederin had been used up, perhaps oxidized and attacked by Dave's own defensive enzymes. Then the wound began to heal just like a regular, heat-induced burn.

This toxic rove beetle is a member of the genus *Paederus*, comprising some six hundred species found around the world but especially prevalent in wet, tropical habitats. *Paederus*'s greatest threat to humans is that its deadly secretion can cause blindness, a common event in areas where mass emergences take place. (The investigators who first purified pederin were able to collect 100 million beetles, the quantity needed to extract enough toxin to perform the chemical analysis, from just one such mass emergence.) Pederin, incidentally, is not all bad as far as humans are concerned. Like many toxins, it has medical value when ju-

diciously applied in tiny amounts. A Chinese manuscript written in the year 739 suggests that it could be used to remove tattoos and to treat boils and ringworm. Further benefits have been confirmed by more recent studies. The application of small amounts to areas of skin with dermatosis, such as eczema and chronic sores and ulcers, especially in older patients, effected complete healing where all other treatments had failed. Perhaps the most original use of this beetle was made by eastern European males who had the intelligence to see that serving in World War I was not adaptive behavior. Collecting two species of *Paederus*, they obtained medical exemptions by using pederin to induce ulcers and inflammations that were hideous and painful but preferable to the effects of grenades, heavy artillery, and mustard gas.

My account of this biochemical horror story is not meant to repel anyone considering a foray into tropical forest; there are plenty of temperate-zone insects that also produce toxic substances. My point is simply an ecological one: it appears to me that the proportion of rainforest insects with chemical defenses is relatively high. There are several reasons why we might expect this to be the case. Some ecologists believe that the ratio of predators to prey and the ecological importance of predation as opposed to other causes of mortality—the weather, for example—are highest in rainforests. As a result, rainforest organisms such as insects would invest relatively greater amounts of their resources in developing and maintaining antipredator chemistry.

A related factor is that many rainforest insects are long lived. Tropical butterflies such as *Heliconius* are known to survive

Many leaf-eating beetles of the family Chrysomelidae, such as this tortoise beetle (*Coptocycla* sp.), are able to store toxic chemicals manufactured by their host plants and employ them for their own defense.

the better part of a year. Such long exposure to predators increases the value of a chemical defense system. By comparison, short-lived insects that have a brief adult stage, like mayflies and midges, lack any chemical defenses.

The true extent of invertebrate defenses is just being unearthed. Only nine hundred beetle species have been chemically surveyed—a tiny fraction of the millions that exist. Yet that small sample has revealed an astonishing repertoire of secretions, a collection of chemical structures with intriguing biological properties. Some beetles produce antifungal and antibacterial compounds such as methyl 8-hydroxyquinoline-2-carboxylate, a dual-purpose secretion that also acts as a predator deterrent by causing intestinal spasms in mice. Other secretions, such as colymbetin, lower the blood pressure of mammals. Bombardier beetles mix quinones and peroxides together and jet out a burning spray that they can direct with great accuracy. The two chemicals are mixed at the point of discharge, producing an explosive heat-generating reaction that sprays out a caustic mixture with a temperature of 212 degrees F (100 degrees C), as hot as boiling water.

Various other beetle secretions rival pederin for potency. Bushmen in the Kalahari use the oral secretion of *Diamphidia simplex* to make poison arrows; the ooze from a single insect can destroy a large mammal. The cantharidin of "Spanish fly" fame is a secretion common in meloid blister beetles and is so highly toxic that the Merck Manual says it causes "severe gastroenteritis, melena, renal damage, haematuria, spermatorrhea, priapism, profound collapse, and death." One wonders what gruesome circumstances yielded this information. At least some of the symptoms were described from a particular case of poisoning. French soldiers stationed in Algiers ate a meal of frogs that had themselves dined on a large number of meloid beetles. The cantharidin had thus made its way up the food chain, and as it passed through the soldiers' digestive systems and urinary tracts, it caused severe disturbances, including *"erections douloureuses et prolongées."* Vertebrate predators, however, are almost certainly not the principal selective force responsible for the evolution of cantharidin.

Male meloids alone synthesize cantharidin, using it as a nuptial gift to females. The compound is transferred to the female during mating. She then coats her eggs with cantharidin as they are laid, so that it functions as an egg protector. Ants are known to be repelled by minute traces of the secretion, and since ants groom leaf surfaces and remove insect eggs, such a transfer benefits both partners quite apart from enhancing their survival.

Few tropical vertebrates possess any significant chemical weaponry. Mammals produce plenty of interesting and complex excretions, but the vast majority are social signals for mate attraction and territorial marking. Skunks are the only mammals with a defense comparable to that of a bombardier beetle. Birds have scarcely any defensive excretions, with the exception of vultures and various seabirds that regurgitate bilious fluids on intruders. Likewise, lizards, turtles, and snakes have few overt chemical defenses. Some snakes and turtles have sour-smelling cloacal discharges, but they lack the irritant authority of many invertebrate-generated molecules. Snake venoms can be a formidable

The red-and-black color of these mating giant millipedes is associated with their ability to produce cyanide-rich defensive secretions.

deterrent, but they are first and foremost feeding adaptations. Only the spitting cobras of Africa and Southeast Asia use venoms for deterrence at a distance.

Most of the chemical defenses found in the rainforest, then, belong to plants and arthropods. They pose a threat only to those intent on browsing at random or to entomologists conditioned by their strange subculture to grab at almost any new specimen without restraint. The average visitor has little to fear from rainforest plants and insects. From time to time, however, almost every tropical naturalist has a purely accidental brush with a well-defended insect.

The last experience I had akin to Dave's burning beetles was also caused by the slightest contact with an insect in Monteverde. I was walking along an overgrown trail through thick second growth on a west-facing slope. The late-afternoon sun was hot, and I had made the mistake of thoughtlessly rolling up my shirt-sleeves. An electrifying prickling on my bare forearm startled me. I looked at my arm but saw nothing. Then a series of red welts began to materialize on the white skin, giving a colorful calligraphic form to the rising wave of torment. I knew what the agency was; the question was, Where were they? One hates to suffer pain and not see the source. I looked behind me at the vegetation. A few feet back, I found them on a small shrub: a cluster of very large and decorative silkmoth caterpillars. The size of small cigars, they were green with red flecks and long, elegantly branched and star-tufted spines. It was the delicate tracery of those spines

that traumatized my skin and left it itching for days after the pain subsided. Caterpillars with irritating hairs are known the world over, but temperate forms usually have only mildly toxic properties. Some tropical families, notably the Megalopygidae, take the stinging defense a step further, having evolved specialized spines that act as hypodermic injectors of potent venom. These beautiful caterpillars look like the antithesis of nastiness.

One common Peruvian species of megalopygid caterpillar is known as the *cuy dorado*, or golden guinea pig. It looks like a tiny furry mammal with a soft, long-haired yet neatly combed coat. But to touch one can be among the world's worst experiences. Underneath the soft hairs are sharp, venom-injecting spines. In addition to histamine, the venom contains proteins that destroy blood cells and tissue. Doctors excel at describing the horrible impact of these compounds, which "begins with stinging, immediately followed by an intense burning pain; a few minutes later, a diffuse area of erythema develops. This area, within 2 to 15 minutes, will show whitish edematous hemispheric papules, about two to three millimeters [about 0.10 inches] in diameter. ... They may coalesce and form an urticarial weal, with a whitish rough surface, which itches violently for one hour or more. Within 24 hours, the lesion will have developed into a congestive and slightly edematous cord showing numerous isolated or coalescent vesicles and sometimes blisters. These later break up, spontaneously or by trauma, and develop into erosions or excoriations that dry up and, five to seven days after the sting, become covered with scabby small crusts." Of course, poison ivy can produce the same sort of horror on one's hide, but victims of these delicate caterpillars vomit and pass out from the pain. Remarkably, that did not prevent various Brazilian tribes from using them to inflame and swell their genitals for recreational purposes.

The bright colors and bold patterns of these insects are no coincidence. Most well-defended insects advertise their unpalatability with a strong form of sign language that discourages birds and other visual predators from pecking at them. One can use this pattern to make some crude judgments about the wisdom of handling an unknown insect. However, even if one avoids touching insects, one can still get burned. A few insect weapons are released even as one approaches and peers at the insect. There are reduviid assassin bugs from Zanzibar that reportedly spray a saliva that is pharmacologically similar to cobra venom. The saliva contains proteins that break down tissue, cause paralysis, and contain hyaluronidase (the enzyme common to snake venoms and leech saliva), which is the "spreading factor" that breaks down tissue and allows the venom to disperse rapidly. Spraying their digestive juices perhaps enables these assassin bugs to deter birds or monkeys that would suffer from an eyeful.

Because of the surprising range of arthropod sprays, one occasionally gets coated with one of them quite unexpectedly. Both millipedes and stink bugs can spray their mixtures of benzaldehyde and hydrogen cyanide for distances of up to about 2 feet (about 0.5 m). For those who enjoy amaretto or almond cookies, the similar smelling scent of these bugs can have delicious and pleasant connotations. But when the substance is applied, it can be horrible. While trying to navigate through a thicket in southern Borneo, I stuck my head down in order to plough through a small archway of vines. As I passed under the vegetation, I got a full dose of the acrid spray of a stink bug, a burning, eye-watering mixture that had an oil-of-almond aroma. Often such secretions contain hydrocarbons and solvents that are designed to allow the caustic toxic compounds to penetrate the skin rapidly. It felt as though my face were being oxidized, and no doubt there would have been skin damage if I had not washed it off.

The mechanism millipedes employ for producing cyanide gas has been elegantly worked out by Tom Eisner, an ecologist who specializes in arthropod defenses. Free cyanide compounds would poison the millipedes themselves if they were stored in active form. Instead, the millipedes—in this case, polydesmids, a group common in the rainforest understory—mix them as needed. The millipede has a series of chambers distributed along its body segments. Each chamber is full of an inert fluid made up of a compound called mandelonitrile. The chamber can be emptied with a muscular squeeze that forces the liquid to the outside by passing it through a smaller chamber. This chamber contains an enzyme that breaks down the mandelonitrile into hydrogen-cyanide gas and benzaldehyde. As the reacting mixture emerges from the body, it produces a protective cloud of toxic gas that surrounds the quiescent millipede for 30 minutes or more.

Many plants produce similar cyanide-generating compounds. Wild sapotes (*Pouteria* spp.), for example, impregnate their green fruits with the cyanide-based prussic acid. If you find one of these avocado-sized fruits while it is still green and slice it open with

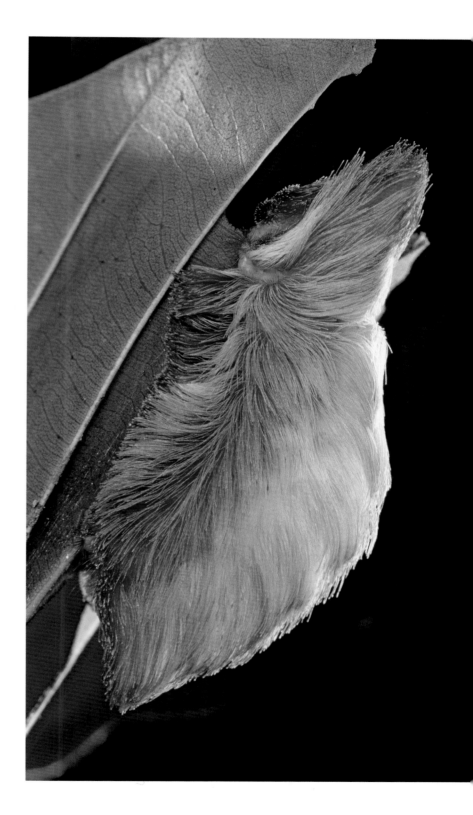

This puss moth caterpillar (*Megalopyge* sp.) looks innocuous, but its furry coat conceals sharp spines that provide a stinging defense. With the slightest contact, the spines break off in the victim's skin, and the toxic chemicals they contain cause instant, excruciating pain.

When molested by a predator, this pericopid moth (*Eucyane drucei*) expels a noxious, foultasting foam from pores on its thorax.

a pocketknife, white fluid oozes from the flesh and the smell of almonds fills the air. The presence of the compound no doubt helps defend the immature seed from attacks by agoutis and other seed-eating rodents. Comparable products are apparently released from the roots of various *Prunus* species (a group with both temperate members—such as peaches and cherries—and tropical species) as an aggressive territorial defense against other plant competitors.

It makes a lot of sense for toxin-generating insects to expel their defensive chemicals in advance of an attack, thus minimizing the risk that a naïve predator will damage the insect with an exploratory peck or a trial tasting. It is not always successful. Eisner reports on a laboratory interaction between a walking stick with a toxic spray and a *Marmosa* mouse opossum, an important insect predator found in Central and South American rainforests. Eisner watched the marmosa attack the walking stick and promptly receive a spray on its muzzle. The irritation was obvious—the marmosa dashed about wiping its face, but all the while, it held on to the walking stick with its paw. Eventually, the spray was exhausted and the marmosa was able to eat the walking stick. Little larger than a shrew, the marmosa has the ferocious appetite required to fuel a small, heat-radiating body, and it will risk noxious irritation to avoid starvation. Eisner also reports that the tiny and voracious grasshopper mouse, another insect specialist with representatives in Central American rainforests, will attack and eat beetles that have toxic sprays.

Perhaps such chemical emissions will not serve for desperate specialists such as mouse opossums, but I know from experience that they work well on larger vertebrates. Not only do some of them irritate the skin, mucous membranes, and eyes, but they

also taste terrible. I have been surprised on several occasions by the chemical defenses of danaid butterflies and pericopid moths. The former are often patterned in oranges and blacks, and the latter are beautiful creatures sporting bold patterns of luminous blues and heavy reds set on a deep navy-blue background. When they are molested, a bubbly froth flows out of the pores in the upper thorax. Once I touched a minuscule dab of this foam to the tip of my tongue and was rewarded with an enduring vile bitterness that lasted for several hours and resisted my efforts to wash it away.

Perhaps the ultimate in chemical repellency over a long distance is a tropical hornet's nest. One is often advised, "If you don't bother them, they won't bother you." Unfortunately, that is not universally true. Many of the seven hundred species of tropical social wasps are docile and attack only when the colony is being ravaged. However, a few species with large colonies and thousands of resident workers have a great deal to lose and can afford to expend a few workers in defense of the colony. Such species will mount an attack even if one stands innocently some distance from the hive. I have been chased off by *Polybia* and assorted *Stelopolybia* wasps when I have been as far as 16 feet (5 m) from the nest. The wasps appear acutely sensitive to the odor of mammalian sweat, and the slightest vibration of their nesting tree sends them swarming. They fly at your head and eyes and, at the moment of impact, turn their abdomen down toward your skin, the better to drive home their barbed stingers. Like honeybee workers, the whole apparatus is designed to leave the stinger securely embedded, with its sac of venom feeding poison into your body. As with most insects, it is not the physical impact but chemistry, a soup of tissue-cleaving enzymes and histamine, that does the discouraging.

Numerous frogs use chemicals as a defense against predators. The most toxic of all is the golden poison dart frog (*Phyllobates terribilis*), which contains enough batrachotoxin—one of the most potent neurotoxins known—to kill about 20,000 mice or 50 humans. A lethal dose from this Colombian endemic causes heart failure.

The coordinated social order and communication systems of these societies are designed to target and apply the venomous defense before the nest can be physically damaged. Often, the sentinel worker wasps on the nest comb will drum their abdomens vigorously on the nest surface, summoning up a frenzy of additional defenders from within. Some of the aerial attackers actually spray venom into the air around you, a release that acts as an alarm signal, identifying the threat and inciting more stinging.

But a specialist predator can circumvent even this group defense. Capuchin monkeys such as *Cebus apella* get almost half their food from hornet nests. Ecologist John Terborgh, who has conducted the longest-running project on neotropical monkey foraging, told me this long ago. But having studied the wasps for several years and having experienced their considerable weaponry, I found it difficult to believe any primate would risk such injury for a fistful of grubs. (My own excuse was that I was after a PhD.) When I visited Terborgh's study site in Peru's Manú Park, however, I saw an astounding case of monkey versus hornet that made me a believer.

I was doing my laundry in the clearing, a grassy yard with a few shrubs surrounded by a wall of forest. A large male capuchin monkey was sitting in a tree, peering down into the clearing. Monkeys pass through the area with great frequency, so I paid it little mind. It moved closer to the clothesline, paused, and leapt out into the clearing, grabbing onto the trunk of a dead *Cecropia* tree. It won a little more of my attention when it began to descend, something monkeys are loath to do in the presence of humans. Once on the ground, it took two quick hops to a shrub and bounded into the air, reaching up with both arms. It came down with a hornet's nest the size of a soccer ball in its hands. A cloud of disoriented wasps poured out as it sprang across the

clearing shaking its prize. In a few seconds, it was working its way through the treetops again.

The monkey had relied on suddenness for its success. No doubt, it received a few stings, but most of the wasps remained swarming confusedly around the shrub. As its reward, the capuchin had many combs packed with tender white larvae. While to me the heist appeared premeditated, practiced, intelligent, and even courageous, the behavioral and ecological significance of the monkey's action was its effectiveness in circumventing the wasps' ability to mount a coordinated defense. Perhaps that is why these hornets often attack first when given the chance. They cannot respond to an unanticipated all-out assault and social disruption. Against such an intelligent predator, the best defense is a discouraging preemptive strike. If you are stung for no apparent reason, you may credit it to that.

Temperate-tropical differences in host-plant defenses may also contribute to the trend toward tropical toxicity. Many herbivorous insects extract poisons from their host plants. Often, insect defensive compounds are nitrogen-rich alkaloids of complex construction. It is well known that the proportion of plants containing alkaloids increases as one moves from the high latitudes toward the equator; proportionately twice as many tropical plants contain alkaloids as do nontropical plants. Why this should be is a matter of guesswork, but perhaps the unrelenting presence and pressure of leaf-eating insects has an impact in the tropics. In the land where winter never comes, there is probably less weather-induced insect mortality than in higher latitudes. In response, tropical plants must invest relatively more in anti-insect defenses.

Insects that specialize in certain plants can develop immunity to defensive compounds and turn them to their own ends, which means that the opportunities for herbivorous insects to sequester defensive alkaloids from plants are greatest in the tropics. Sometimes, as in the case of *Paederus*, the insect synthesizes its own toxins. This is especially true for the many arthropods, including carpenter ants, various caterpillars, and vinegarroons, that use simple compounds such as formic and acetic acid (vinegar). Often, herbivorous insects use their host plants as a source of chemical weaponry.

The squash and cucumber family, a primarily tropical one of about eight hundred species of sprawling and climbing vines, affords a classic example. One can often find a vine of some sort in tree-fall gaps that clearly resembles a small cucumber or squash. Do not taste the fruit; most are laced with various oxygenated tetracyclic triterpenes, more commonly known as cucurbitacins. Our domesticated cucumber is edible only because one of our ancestors living in the forests of India discovered and husbanded fruits with few of these defensive compounds. Cucurbitacin is the most bitter substance known. It is detectable by humans at concentrations as low as one part per billion. Accidentally tasting a well-defended wild cucumber fruit can cause a person to collapse with nausea and to suffer severe cramps and diarrhea for days. A minuscule dose, a millionth of a mammal's body weight, can be fatal.

The evolutionary integration of cucurbitacins by some ancestral cucumber was no doubt one of the keys to the success of this plant family. One might expect such an adaptation to allow an ancestral species to become widespread and subsequently speciated during the epoch in which the plants were relatively immune to herbivory. But all good defenses are eventually breached. Certain beetles have accomplished the feat and are now positively attracted to the taste and odor of these compounds. Cucumber beetles outdo even our response to these molecules, exceeding the sensitivity of the most sophisticated chemical-survey techniques. Not only are these elegant black-and-yellow-striped beetles immune to the toxic properties of cucurbitacins, but they actually load up on them. That is why cucumber beetles can become agricultural pests; their ability to consume plant toxins prevents most predators from attacking them. And as specialists on cucurbits, they have relatively little competition from more generalized herbivores.

Plants also produce defensive hormones, but most appear to be directed against the physiology of insects. Many ferns and conifers create compounds that are closely related to the growth and molting hormones of insects, in effect causing a hormonal imbalance that makes it impossible for the insects to grow. If this sounds rather sophisticated for a plant, that is because it is. Plants can neither run nor hide from their predators, and in response to grazing pressure, they have evolved a remarkable array of chemical defenses. In addition to being hydrogen-cyanide generators and hormone mimics, plants are also impregnated with tannin and phenols that inhibit digestion, vast numbers of poisonous alkaloids, relatives of mustard gas, opiates, saponin, hallucinogens, vitamin- and protein-destroying enzymes, and essential oils that destroy beneficial gut bacteria. Plants contain as much molecular weaponry as insects do, yet we pass by them in the forest, unaware of the toxic presence hidden in greenery.

There are, however, significant exceptions. Tropical nettles can be unforgiving of even the slightest contact. In a remarkable convergence with stinging caterpillars, nettle hairs are laced with histamine, which causes a massive allergic reaction, and with acetylcholine, which is involved in carrying impulses through the nervous system. Presumably, the latter aids in firing the skin's network of pain receptors. I have been stung by both northern nettles and tropical nettles. There is no doubt that the latter group, which includes some species with conspicuous red spines, is better at inducing loud cursing and dancing in the careless.

Often, the toxicity of a plant is correlated with the appearance and toxicity of the insects that feed on it. Many tropical plants in the milkweed, Apocynaceae, Euphorbiaceae, and Moraceae families are protected by a white, chemically toxic sap, and these plants often cater to insect herbivores that are warningly colored and presumably chemically defended. A common hazard in New World rainforests is a tree known appropriately as *Sapium*. It is found in second growth and forest edges of montane rainforest, the sort of spot where one flails indiscriminately with a machete to clear a passage. When *Sapium* is cut, it immediately exudes large amounts of white sap capable of causing blindness if even a single droplet lands in an eye.

Insects that feed on the white-sapped plants are often brilliantly marked with warning colors. The large and conspicuous sphinx moth feeds on frangipani (*Plumeria rubra*). This bold black-and-red-striped caterpillar shows every sign of being unpalatable and is markedly different in coloration and behavior from other sphingid caterpillars. It feeds in the open by day, in contrast to most of its relatives, which are nocturnal, cryptic, and apparently palatable. Birds are known to eat these caterpillars, and I have watched a big male *Cebus apella* monkey find a large cryptic sphingid and proceed to eat it with obvious pleasure, biting the tough head capsule off and sucking the contents out of the skin. But when these same monkeys find brilliantly patterned sphingids, which often mass on tree trunks, they avoid them and even express what the primatologists who study them describe as alarm calls.

Sometimes, rainforest plants with white sap are not at all toxic. People drink white sap from "milk trees," the name of various *Brosimum* species in the fig family. *Brosimum* trees were among the rainforest trees especially guarded by the Mayas who managed tracts of forest in the Yucatán Peninsula and the Petén region of Guatemala. We make chewing gum out of the milky sap of *Manilkara* trees, the "chicle" trees that were also selectively maintained in Mayan forests. In this case, the sap is still defensive in function, although it works not by chemical damage but by physical obstruction, acting as a gum or glue that makes feeding on it impossible. Rubber is a result of the interaction between a euphorb tree and the herbivores that attempt to breach its bark.

Some arthropods also rely on tacky expulsions for defense. The onychophorans (*Peripatus*, for example), caterpillar-like animals that patrol the leaf litter of rainforests, are a primitive crossover between annelid worms and arthropods. They are predators on relatively large, mobile prey such as crickets and roaches. Truly peripatetic, onychophorans are no match for a bounding cricket or a flying roach. Instead, they snare their prey with a squirt of proteinaceous glue. These same strands of sticky cement are used to fend off attacking ants.

Male ithomiine butterflies, like this transparent glasswing butterfly (*Greta oto*), form leks where they compete to attract females. The leks are maintained with the aid of pheromones derived from alkaloids collected from a variety of plants, including this yellow daisy (*Lasianthea fruticosa*).

In some cases, adult insects actually go out and collect defensive compounds from plants. The beautiful ithomiine butterflies gather their defensive compounds as adults rather than as larvae, a somewhat surprising method since ithomiines in the caterpillar stage feed almost exclusively on nightshades. One might expect them to gather defensive compounds from their larval host plants, since nightshades are among the most alkaloid-rich families known, giving us nicotine and many pharmaceutically potent alkaloids and hallucinogens. But, for some reason, these butterflies pursue their alkaloids as adults. Ithomiines, especially males, visit various composites and borages whose nectar contains pyrrolizidine alkaloids. Butterfly collectors have long known that one good way to collect masses of male ithomiines is to hang out bunches of dried heliotrope plants rich in these alkaloids. Certain plants, favoring selective and efficient pollination by butterflies, secrete the compounds into their flower nectar, making it repellent to bees, ants, and wasps.

Male ithomiines concentrate the alkaloids in patches of scent scales on their upper forewings, which they expose when sitting on a sunny leaf. The courtship function of the scales seems obvious, and females of some related butterflies are known to be attracted by the presence of these alkaloids in male sexual pheromones. Ecologist Bill Haber believes that the alkaloids in the male scent scales may also be the attraction mechanism causing the formation of ithomiine leks, diffuse aggregations of hundreds of individuals and up to thirty species that fly and display together in the understory. The fact that the alkaloid-laced butterflies are repellent to birds enhances the value of such aggregation for butterflies that are courting and mating. Each mating lek can be considered a giant Müllerian mimicry complex advertising the toxicity of its members.

In Monteverde, I have visited two such leks in stretches of steep-sided riparian forest. Month after month, the butterflies were there in the same spot. They used a variety of warning color patterns. Some species were of soft golden translucence; others had bold tiger stripes of orange and black or black and yellow bars. Many were transparent, all but invisible except when their glassy wings were flecked with sunlight. The lek had a languid air. The butterflies circled around and around, indifferent to my presence, delicate and evanescent but unafraid. The males alternately paused spread-eagled on leaves, then flew up in courtship pursuits, only to eddy back with slow, placid wingbeats. In their tranquil floating flight was the sign of the protective alkaloid gathered from the bittersweet nectar of flowers.

Perhaps an hour amid such an ithomiine aggregation is the best way to appreciate the virtues of defensive toxins. Such molecules bring not just pain or caution into the naturalist's experience of rainforests. They are the invisible progenitors of great beauty.

El tigre
Why jaguars are the ultimate predator

He has coughed in the night outside my tent in Peru, a throaty sound that raises primordial hackles, turns full the heart's pounding throttle, and sends a squeeze of adrenaline into the arteries. The ears crackle with reborn awareness of the forest noises outside; the mind wonders if the rustle in the leaf litter is his careful tread. While plodding the muddy pampas in Bolivia, I have stopped and looked around wide-eyed at fresh, wet prints, each as large as my face. But for me, he remains an invisible presence. I have yet to see *el tigre* in the flesh.

Jaguar signs are here and there in neotropical forests, but *el tigre* is always thinly spread and encountered only by people who are either diligent or lucky. Those who are both have the best chance of all. Yet if the jaguar is glimpsed only sporadically, it is nevertheless perpetually present in the lives of the animals and in the minds and cultures of the people who live in the rainforest.

The largest, most powerful predator in the neotropical forest, *Panthera onca*, or *Felis onca*, as some systematists call it, lives at the top of the trophic pyramid. The biomass of a single jaguar, weighing up to 350 pounds (160 kg), represents the end point for thousands of other lives, from plant to insect and small mammal and bird, fish, and reptile, into this final magnificent feline form.

This cat, this spotted panther, is a geographic generalist. The only New World member of the genus *Panthera*, the jaguar ranges all the way from the southwestern United States to Argentina. It prowls in coastal rainforests and roams all the way to the edge

Jaguar populations are declining in part because the attractive spotted pelt of this cat is still widely sought by poachers. But loss of adequate habitat is the greatest threat to the survival of this wide-ranging predator.

of the tree line in the Andes. No natural competitor is powerful enough to restrict the foraging excursions of this cat.

What does a jaguar eat? Everything it can. Or so it seems. Mammalogist Louise Emmons, working in Peru, observed that jaguars kill and eat almost any vertebrate they encounter, except perhaps adult tapirs, which may be difficult to take down. The tapir's technique for dealing with a jaguar foolish enough to leap aboard is to crash blindly through dense vegetation until a stout limb sweeps the jaguar off. Theodore Roosevelt, who had a fascination for that sort of phenomenon, noted that "the tapir is no respecter of timber."

Jaguars take even white-lipped peccary, in spite of that group's formidable social defense. Herds of white-lips usually number fifty to a hundred animals. Compact, powerful creatures with large, slashing teeth, they charge an intruder from all sides when attacked or threatened and could easily wound or kill a cat on the ground. The jaguar's strategy is to wait in a tree for the herd to pass by, quickly drop down upon a single peccary, kill it with a neck bite, then leap back into the tree. Crouching on a branch several feet (1 to 2 m) above the ground puts the jaguar well beyond the reach of the pigs. The alarmed pigs have nothing to attack, and the jaguar is later able to descend and feed on its prey. If the animal is light enough, the jaguar may carry it into the tree immediately. But white-lip herds are seminomadic and not predictably available prey. The large cat must therefore use other foraging tactics as well.

Game is rarely concentrated in rainforests the way it is at African water holes or around winter deeryards in North America. So the jaguar spends much of its time on the prowl, waiting for random encounters with a great variety of potential prey items. It is one of the few neotropical mammals that is about equally

Although many carnivorous mammals are primarily nocturnal, the jaguar hunts by both night and day. By day, its spotted coat provides camouflage in the mottled sun and shade of the rainforest undergrowth in which it hunts.

active day and night, perhaps a reflection of the dietary breadth it requires. Surveying scat samples, Emmons found that jaguars take both diurnal and nocturnal animals, including squirrels, opossums, rodents like paca and capybara, deer, monkeys, and birds, as well as grass and something she lists as "unidentified scaly lumps." Only the peccary seems to be taken more often than a random walk would suggest.

Surprise is a crucial element of the hunt and is no doubt the reason the jaguar has a spotted coat that camouflages it in the forest's mottle of light and shade. (There is a rare black form of the jaguar that closely resembles an Asian black panther, a form that would seem well adapted for hunting by night.) The hunting jaguar's task is to see before being seen. In this, it is aided by the large, forward-set eyes typical of the big cats, which give them

great depth perception in the range of 50 to 80 feet (15 to 25 m) and stereoscopic vision beyond that, distances that a jaguar can cover in a few quick bounds. The rest is over quickly. Unlike the slightly smaller and more delicate puma with which it coexists, the jaguar has remarkable crushing power in its bite. Its massive skull gives this cat an almost square-headed look—the result of the zygomatic arches of bone that flare out from each side of its head to accommodate the huge muscles running from the anchor site, a large sagittal crest of bone astride the skull. The muscles power a set of heavy jaws equipped with stout canines. Ecologist Richard Kilte has calculated the bite force of the jaguar to be about 150 percent greater than that of a puma and as much as 10 times that of smaller cats like margays, which is why the jaguar can eat animals such as caimans. Anyone who has grabbed even a tiny live specimen of these strong, durably plated reptiles will recognize that taking such a creature in the mouth and swallowing it ranks as a notable gastronomic accomplishment.

The jaguar is a water-loving cat and catches a considerable portion of its food there. Emmons radio-collared and tracked jaguars and found that they spent much time hunting along the river's edge, where they would snag, wrestle, kill, and eat resting caimans. The jaguar is also reported by other observers to fish for tambaqui, a large characoid piranha that eats fruit, by taking up a post on a limb over the water and tapping on the surface in imitation of falling fruit. When the fish rises to investigate, the cat snags it with its claws. This aquatic preference and the jaguar's ability to feed on tough prey appear to be the major differences between jaguars and pumas.

Reptiles such as turtles and crocodiles were once an abundant resource in Amazonia and the Orinoco drainage; the sandbars and beaches used to swarm with nesting *Podocnemis* turtles. Humboldt wrote about the turtle nestings that produced millions of eggs—so many, in fact, that the harvests that used to sustain both Indians and jaguars were taken over by the Jesuit and Franciscan missionaries. They massed the eggs in dugouts, boiled off the oil, and exported the resulting *manteca de tortugas*, or turtle lard, to Europe, consuming in the process some 33 million eggs annually from one section of the Orinoco. Predictably, the turtle populations are now devastated, but Humboldt recorded that "a great number of these animals are devoured by jaguars the moment they leave the water" and was disconcerted to find that not even fires would keep the jaguars away from his campsites along the turtle beaches. He noted that in order to devour the turtles at their ease, the jaguars "turn them so that the under shell is uppermost. In this situation, the turtles cannot rise; and as the jaguar turns many more than he can eat in one night, the Indians often avail themselves of his cunning and avidity."

Although the jaguar is able to use its long claws and paws to pull a river turtle from its shell, access to much of the reptilian resource depends on the jaguar's uniquely powerful bite. The most impressive evidence of the jaguar's jaw power I have seen is in its handling of the land tortoise's shell.

Around the area where Emmons worked at Cocha Cashu in Peru's Manú Biosphere Reserve, there is a healthy population of the ground-dwelling tortoise *Geochelone denticulata*. This tortoise is hefty, weighing about 9.7 pounds (4.4 kg). Its protective plastron and carapace are solid bone that appears sturdy enough to resist an attack with a hammer. But on my first visit to Cocha Cashu, I was surprised to see a huge pile of partially demolished *Geochelone* shells. The pile had been collected by biologists working in the area. The shells, which are about as long as a football, invariably looked as though they had been treated like a huge, armor-plated hamburger, with the jaguar simply taking the shell in its mouth and biting right through the side of it with what must be a tremendous bone-cracking, shell-splintering crunch. One inevitably concludes that a jaguar would find the human skull about as challenging as a ripe cantaloupe. For its size, no cat bites harder than *el tigre*.

Panthera onca is a creature with a reputation for possessing little fear of humans. Records of attacks on humans are numerous. The Jesuit missionary Eder, who wrote of life in eastern Bolivia in the years prior to 1772, had enough information at hand to give a detailed chronology of the way in which a jaguar dispatches humans, beginning with an attack to the head, followed by consumption of the throat region and great attention to the consequent outpouring of blood from the large arteries, which it carefully licked up "in order not to lose a single drop." (This is an approach that all the big cats seem to use when taking down

Among the jaguar's dietary mainstays are relatively large mammals such as the collared peccary, top, and the red brocket deer, bottom, both of which are common in the rainforest.

prey large enough to require a suffocating throat bite rather than a severing bite to the back of the neck.) Perhaps that fearlessness and power to threaten, coupled with the role of top predator, which it shares with humans of the rainforest, explain the jaguar's dominant presence in the mythology of the forest tribes of Central and South America.

Anthropologist Janet Suskind explains the anthropomorphic appeal the jaguar holds for the Sharanahua of Brazil and Peru: "Ordinary game was taken with bows and arrows, but men and jaguars were killed with spears. Jaguars, like men, are predators, the only important predators in the tropical forest. In a real sense, jaguars are competitors for meat . . . . because he is a competitor, the jaguar, like all strangers, is dangerous and should be killed before he attacks." So, too, the Desana of Colombia recognize the ecological role of the jaguar. Of all the animals in the forest, only the jaguar is not subservient to the spiritual "master of the animals." Instead, it is acclaimed as a resourceful hunter and is represented symbolically as "a fertilizing force derived directly from the sun."

When Amazonian Indians use hallucinogenic vehicles to explore and divine fate and the future, they often rendezvous with *el tigre*. Manuel Cordova, a native Peruvian, describes how under the influence of ayahuasca, or yage (the extract of *Banisteriopsis* vines), visits with jaguars, sometimes black ones, were traditional: "My sensing faculties became those of the black animals. Sight, sound, smell, feel, and instinct were tuned in with those of this most astute beast of the forest. And we prowled together—investigating dark, hidden things beyond the ken of uninitiated man, unexplainable in his language." Ethnobotanist Richard Evans Schultes, who lived with Amazonian Indians and explored their hallucinogenic rituals, writes that along with snakes, jaguars dominate the visions, "since they are the only beings respected and feared by the Indians of the tropical forest; because of their power and stealth, they have assumed a place of primacy in aboriginal religious beliefs. In many tribes, the shaman becomes a feline during the intoxication, exercising his powers as a cat." The relationship is reflected in the fact that in many Indian languages, the same word is used to mean shaman and jaguar.

Jaguar cults abound in pre-Columbian neotropical culture from Mexico south to Brazil. In the most remote forests of Amazonia, where shotguns have not replaced spears, necklaces of jaguar claws and teeth remain the hunter's emblem of valor. Many of these cultures are now extinct, but the jaguar's face continues to stare out from carvings, friezes, and glyphs on temples in Mexico and along the Peruvian coastal desert. A jaguar stalks in a highly stylized way across a Chorotega Indian ceramic I bought, a newly made piece sold along a paved highway in Costa Rica. The Olmecs, Zapotecs, Aztecs, Mayas, Chavíns, and Incas all gave *el tigre* a place at the top of their spiritual pantheon of gods.

But where is the jaguar's place now in the cultures of Latin America? Humans, the competitors and predators of jaguars, have succeeded in reducing their numbers throughout most of the jaguar's natural range. It is easy for an animal that roams over areas as large as 16,000 acres (6,500 hectares) to run out of room. In Monteverde, Costa Rica, jaguars have rebounded following increased protection of forest and wildlife. But the for-

The jaguar is the largest terrestrial predator in the New World rainforest. Heavy jaws with a massive set of muscles give it a wide, rounded face and one of the most powerful bites of any cat.

In addition to hunting large mammals, the jaguar preys opportunistically on many smaller species, including the Central American agouti (*Dasyprocta punctata*).

est that remains is a ragged island, which is only about 247,000 acres (100,000 hectares) in area. All around it are cattle and dairy farms. The killing of cattle by jaguars is on the increase.

In Monteverde, the local conservation league where I sometimes work was notified by forest guards and farmers about three incidents of jaguar attacks that destroyed a bull, a cow, and a horse, all in different localities. We did not know how many jaguars were involved, but we knew that if nothing else were done, the farmers' reaction would be to run dogs on the jaguars, tree the wild cats, and shoot them. Because the jaguar population was limited to perhaps five to twenty individuals, we decided to compensate the farmers for their losses in return for their agreement not to kill the offending jaguars should they show themselves. The money could have been used to protect more habitat, but that protection would have been at the cost of jaguar lives. The only alternative was to try to locate and tranquilize the jaguars and move them to a new site. Few people have the skill to manage such an operation without considerable risk to the animals. But our greatest problem was not technology; it was space. Officials at several nearby national parks refused to accommodate any jaguars. They, too, were running at capacity, and moving animals around is one way to spread disease. In fact, Costa Rica has almost run out of habitat that might absorb *el tigre*.

In countries such as Costa Rica, jaguars may be among what tropical ecologist Dan Janzen calls "the living dead," animals whose needs for space are so great that their populations are already too small and too thinly spread. Although they still exist, the living dead are irrevocably headed for extinction in those areas that lack the huge amounts of land needed to sustain genetically viable, non-inbred populations.

It is an understandable temptation to give up on something that is labeled a member of the living dead. But the concept should do more than simply allow us to relegate animals such as the jaguar to the category of extinction and to focus our attention on less demanding species. Instead, it highlights the necessity of fighting hardest for those areas that are still large enough to sustain the jaguar in its natural state. These cats are what is known as an "umbrella species." With their popular appeal, they are able to attract strong public support, and if enough space is saved for the jaguar, a huge amount of habitat for the lower echelons of living creatures is also guaranteed. And only a system like this contains the true ecological character and full complement of the rainforest.

Jaguars and other cats such as ocelots are "keystone predators." This means that one of the functions they perform is the regulation of the abundance of some of the more prolific rodents. There is a dichotomy in the reproductive rates of rainforest mammals. Many herbivorous mammals, especially seed-eating rodents like agoutis, peccaries, and capybaras, have large litters. The small rodents are even more fecund. Emmons has found that ocelots, for example, cropped these small rodents at a correspondingly tremendous rate, removing 69 percent of the annual production, while jaguars consumed peccaries, coatimundis, capybaras, and others in proportion to their abundance and at a much lower rate overall.

Ecologist John Terborgh suggests that these two predators have a strong regulating effect because they have either a high cropping rate, as in the case of ocelots, or one that is tied to prey abundance—that is, the most numerous animals are those most frequently eaten by jaguars. He found support for this thesis when he compared densities of these herbivores in areas of Peru, where the cat populations remain healthy, with those in areas like Panama, where cats have been annihilated. In Panama, incidentally, the well-studied field site Barro Colorado Island has elevated levels of opossums, armadillos, and rabbits and has ten times as many animals such as agoutis and coatimundis as do the areas that retain large predator populations. In other words, removal of the top-level predators did not cause the collapse of the trophic pyramid. But it did result in a major shift in proportions, destroying communities of common herbivore species such as the rodents.

The eventual outcome of this shift is not easy to predict, because the effects may not be evident for a century. For example, agouti and peccary abundance may destroy the ability of palm trees to reseed, thereby reducing the recruitment of young palm seedlings into the forest. In addition to sustaining important food animals such as peccaries, macaws, and rodents, palms are keystone resources for the indigenous people of Amazonia. Of all plants, the palm family is universally rated as the most important, being a source of oils, fruits rich in vitamins, high-protein nuts, waterproof and fiber thatching for houses, and the best wood for bows and arrows. Fewer cats means more agoutis, which means fewer palms, which in turn means fewer peccaries and even fewer cats. If the interaction continues long enough, we lose the cats, but ultimately the palms might go as well, followed by the agoutis and peccaries. The symbolic importance of the jaguar in mythic lore may be more vital and appropriate than we will ever realize.

Jaguars themselves have no predators other than humans; before the advent of guns, they were abundant. But despite their appeal, jaguars are still being killed at great rates. During zoologist Alan Rabinowitz's two-year study of jaguars in Belize, all six of his study animals died. But pristine jaguar populations can still be found.

The last time I was in Manú, I saw a jaguar skull someone had picked up in the forest. The animal had apparently died of old age, its teeth worn down to mere stubs; perhaps it spent its last days searching for snakes, fish, and other easily swallowed prey. One might find such a prospect a bit grim and sad, but I did not. That skull was concrete evidence of something magnificent: a place where a jaguar can grow old enough to wear down its powerful teeth, where a jaguar can hunt and not be hunted, where a jaguar can walk its way across its full life span, the measure given freely before the age of guns, poachers, and fur traders. As the days of the living dead dawn in more and more countries, we must treasure those places where this regal cat can still lie down to die, possessed of all its allotted days. In such a place, I can wait patiently for my chance to see a jaguar. As long as *el tigre* walks, the spirit of wilderness remains in the forest.

Along the shores of rivers and lakes, jaguars prey heavily on reptiles such as the spectacled caiman (*Caiman crocodilus*), top, and yellow-spotted sideneck turtle (*Podocnemis unifilis*), bottom. The diet of a jaguar seems to reflect the relative availability of prey rather than any specialization.

Beyond the gun

A journey into virgin Amazonia

My companions on a journey made in the late 1980s to Manú, the largest national park on Earth, were a typically ragged-looking handful of field biologists—a mix of Peruvians, Princetonians, and Canadians. We left the high altitudes of Cuzco, Peru, in a truck loaded with the several tons of paraphernalia necessary for a trip into tropical rainforest—giant hooks for catfish, small ones for piranha, thousands of crackers in airtight tins, drums of kerosene, kayaks, and beer—and headed toward one of the few truly pristine regions of the tropics, a trackless land where the wildlife roams unhunted and indigenous peoples still live free in the untamed vastness of eastern Amazonia. It was an experience that completely altered my understanding of the well-worn phrase "virgin forest."

Manú sprawls over the southeastern corner of Peru, running from the edge of the cold altiplano high above the tree line, dropping 11,500 feet (3,500 m) across the slopes of the Andes and spreading into the Amazonian lowlands. It is now officially designated as Manú Biosphere Reserve, a protected area that encompasses 4.4 million acres (1.8 million hectares). The great area harbors more than 1,000 bird species, 1,500 kinds of plants, and over 200 types of mammals, including 13 species of monkeys. Manú is probably the most biologically diverse preserve on Earth, and much of the park is still a biological *terra incognita*.

As our truck crawled up the serpentine mountain road, I began to understand why Manú remains a new, unspoiled world. Intimidating chasms began yawning below the truck soon after

Clouds and mist move over the Quiros Gorge in eastern Ecuador, left. The east slope of the Andes is precipitous, dissected by deep gorges, and covered with lush forests that are home to rare and spectacular species such as the spectacled bear, mountain tapir, and Andean cock-of-the-rock.

we left the Sacred Valley of the Incas and headed over the eastern flank of the Andes. The road was a one-way affair, a narrow slice with barely an inch for human error and too slender to permit two-way traffic. Instead, travel reverses direction every second day.

Much of the single lane was hemmed in on one side by jagged rock walls and on the other by empty sky. Nevertheless, Andean truckers make the most of gravity. Condemned to crawl up steep slopes, they compensate when going downhill, sending their heavily loaded, bald-tired charges careening around blind hairpin turns, accompanied by whining brakes and muttered appeals to Providence from the riders. Often, the drivers fortify themselves against the cold and chasms with an excess of that potent alcoholic hooch Peruvians call *pisco*.

Unfortunately, the one-way rule is often bent. There is always some maniac in a hurry, with a bribe for the guard at the road entrance and a willingness to risk his life and the lives of others to make the trip in the wrong direction. One such reprobate came looming out of the dusk at us. Luckily, there was room to back up, pull over, and allow him to go on into the dark against the grain.

At one point, I saw the sobering roadside crosses that mark the failures of the system. Leaning out over the side of the truck and staring down into the late-afternoon shadows, I could see, hundreds of yards below on the rocks, a splattering of truck doors, wheels, and debris. And I had heard that the park service had recently lost a truck and two men who had dropped over the side farther ahead on the road, a fact that one tried mentally to bury but that resurfaced with every lurching curve.

Alpacas, peasants walking barefoot on the cold, stony soil, and the great sweep of the tussock grass marked our passage above the 13,000-foot (4,000 m) level. High in the treeless al-

Much of the Amazonian rainforest is accessible only by river. The remote backwaters, beyond the reach of motorized boats, remain a haven for ecologically vulnerable species, such as the giant river otter, and a last refuge of the indigenous human inhabitants of tropical rainforests.

tiplano, the first boundary marker of the park appeared as dusk came on. The sky turned from a deep purple to a night sky so cold and clear and black that it felt as if we had passed along the very edge of the atmosphere and into space. A retreat into sleeping bags, and sleep was on. Hours later, I awoke with a face wet from the mist, and we began our descent into the zone of moss-festooned cloud forest.

Even in the gloom, I could see that the cloud forest remained intact, a welcome contrast to much of the Andes where the land has been cleared for coca plantations. Andean cloud-forest plants are distinguished by one of the world's highest degrees of endemism, the localized occurrence of unique species. Often, each set of ridges supports many plants that grow there and nowhere else. The densely matted, damp tangle of habitat, a zone Peruvians refer to as the *ceja de montaña*, the eyebrows of the mountains, is home to little-known wildlife. Spectacled bears climb and clamber here, pulling bromeliads from branches to eat. The cow-sized, woolly-coated mountain tapir, relatively unstudied in spite of its bulk, travels deeply rutted trails and centuries-old routes along ridges beyond human penetration.

At midnight, we stopped for food and bladder relief in an isolated hamlet, the one-shack town of Piowata. We sat on benches and listened as a battery-powered radio blasted out the rhythmic and appropriately mournful *huayno* music of the Andes. Red-eyed guinea pigs scurried nervously underfoot, as if antici-

The Brazilian tapir is the largest terrestrial mammal found in the New World rainforest. Prized for its meat, it is often hunted to extinction around areas of dense human settlement. Parks such as Manú, which sustain small numbers of indigenous inhabitants who traditionally hunt for subsistence needs, are able to maintain healthy tapir populations.

pating that they would soon be the next feature on the menu. John Terborgh, the Princeton ecologist and Manú veteran who had planned the trip, could finally relax. His huge, broad smile gleamed in the lantern light as he looked around and exclaimed, "This is the real Peru."

To many North Americans, the real Peru is an Andean tragedy, a place of agricultural landscapes, deserts, and mountains, a worn-out country that has seen the Inca civilization replaced by tragic combinations: the lucrative cocaine trade mixed with utter poverty, guerrilla warfare and militarism, great resources and great waste. We had seen all of that in Cuzco and Lima—in machine-gun-toting police on every corner, in the newspapers' daily chronicle of violence, in the blood-red political slogans of hate on every street, and in the squalid alleys lined by adobe walls capped with broken bottles. But beyond the coastal cities, beyond the heavily settled Andean plateaus, there are still small, simple villages and, beyond them, Amazonian wilderness. The real Peru for a biologist is that land still free from the pressing density of humanity.

Madre de Dios Province, where the park is located, has only one inhabitant per 247 acres (100 hectares), and most people are found in the town of Puerto Maldonado, near the Brazilian-Bolivian border. Yet true wilderness is not easily found even in this part of Peru. "Much of Amazonia," says Terborgh, "is a hollow shell as far as the animals are concerned. The forest is there, but hunters and trappers have bagged the big cats, the monkeys, the macaws, the caimans, and the giant otters." Manú is an ex-

ception, one of the few places where one can study ecological communities that are unaltered by human influence. The heart of Manú re-creates the time when gunshot blasts or even the puffing of blowguns and the twang of bowstrings were unknown sounds to the parrots, monkeys, tapirs, and peccaries.

To get beyond the range of the shotgun takes almost a week of travel. Terborgh and others like him make the trip out of necessity. As I had learned on the mountain roads, the journey is filled with hazards and difficulties. Terborgh and his students have had boats full of gear stolen; trees have crashed down on them, sinking them in awkward circumstances; and leishmaniasis, a fly-transmitted microorganism that eats hideous leprosy-like ulcers in one's anatomy, has infected Terborgh several times. Leishmaniasis ulcers appear unpredictably, often months after exposure, erupting anywhere on the body. They grow steadily larger if left untreated. A month-long series of injections with antimony compounds is required to halt the microorganism's progress. The treatment strains the liver, tires the victim, and makes the joints ache, and even when vanquished, leishmaniasis often leaves a legacy of disfiguring scars. In Cuzco, we had seen many destitute Indians with noses and faces eaten away by the disease.

We entered the lowlands, and the road, a rocky bed built up during an era of unsuccessful oil exploration, became hemmed in with vegetation. The song of an undescribed species of antbird caught Terborgh's attention, and we scanned the trees for a glimpse of it, all the while trying to duck out of the reach of the dangling hooked lengths of bamboo brushing over the truck.

The oxbow lakes of Manú National Park, left, are shallow, nutrient-rich, and highly productive aquatic ecosystems. When used at low intensity by indigenous inhabitants, they provide an abundance of protein while sustaining healthy populations of black caiman, giant otter, waterfowl, and fish.

Although black caimans (*Melanosuchus niger*), right, feed on fish, they also feed on many terrestrial animals. By defecating into the water, the caimans transfer nutrients from the land, thus stimulating algal production, which in turn results in high ecological productivity. Fishermen may harvest more fish in the presence of caimans than they would without them.

On one trip, Terborgh's ear was torn in two by the once graceful limbs. Nevertheless, we were all gaping at the rich lowland flora as we passed by. As we rolled hour after hour through forest, we did not see a solitary monkey or mammal of any kind. No macaws brightened the sky.

The first European explorers of the New World tropics invariably made similar observations on the scarcity of game. Historian William Prescott, writing about the conquest of Peru, summed up the conquistadors' impression of the "funereal forests," stating that "even brute creation appeared instinctively to have shunned the spot, and neither beast nor bird was seen by the wanderers." Cornel Whiffen, explorer of the northwest Amazon, echoed these remarks, as did Henry Bates and other naturalists before him. The trip, like most others I had made to tropical forests, was so far confirming the impression that animal populations are relatively low in tropical rainforests. I was to change my mind a few days later.

By midmorning, we had successfully forded the Carbon River and had reached the end of the road at Shintuya, a village of acculturated Indians. We watched gold miners buying supplies, a couple of trucks taking on squared-off mahogany logs and the usual cadre of gaunt dogs and swine half-heartedly prospecting for garbage and human excrement.

Our highway was now the Río Alto Madre de Dios, a river whose name might read majestically as the Upper River of the Mother of God. The Alto Madre proved to be a braided, gravelly propellant, spilling cold and clear out of the mountains and running swiftly over the rocky bars, swerving around islands of flood-swept trees and debris. Our craft, a narrow wooden boat of *Cedrela* planks, made rapid time, slithering past the sunken trees and scraping over boulders. My expectations began to rise as we saw flocks of blue-green parakeets swirl like clouds of coordinated living confetti, and from time to time, blue-and-yellow macaws passed in pairs overhead. By nightfall, we reached the confluence of the Manú River, a typically sluggish, yellow-brown Amazonian river that we would ascend for two days.

Before the sun has fully risen, there are two glorious hours of pale rose and then yellow-tinted light, when the mist trails in wisps and eddies along the water, and when wildlife still lurks and stalks and sings along the banks and beaches. But as soon as the sun climbs above the treetops, the water glares painfully, like a rippling mirror, ever shifting to catch and force your eyes away. The landscape of forest, bank, and beach is bleached to flat greens, washed-out browns, and white. Joseph Conrad, who traveled the rivers of Southeast Asia, wrote of "the monotony of the inanimate brooding sunshine of the tropics," and it is true that under its brilliance, much of the wildlife wilts away into the shady forest interior.

The traveler's boat, as often as not, is powered by a belching diesel or, on the smaller tributaries, by a thumping *peque-peque*, the onomatopoeic name for a contraption consisting of a 16-horsepower 4-cycle motor driving an improvised shaft that protrudes far back behind the boat. A craft thus powered makes only modest progress as it zigzags back and forth, working up the sinuous path of the river. The pace of travel is somnolent, the green wall of vegetation is mute, save for the narcotic whine

Buttress roots are a common feature of large trees in the Amazonian rainforest. There has been much speculation about their function, but it seems most likely that they help support the tree, particularly in poorly drained soils.

and drone of cicadas, and it is rarely long before a number of devotedly sanguinary black flies pick up the scent of the captive passengers and crew. Under such circumstances, the veteran of tropical river travel often pulls a hat over the face and hunkers down, retreating into torpidity.

At the guard post controlling access to the interior of the park, we were surprised to encounter a group of Yora Indians, one of several tribes that find refuge in Manú. The area has an ethnic diversity that matches its biological diversity. Piro, Machiguenga, Yora, Amahuaca, Asháninca, Huachipari, Mascho Piro, Amarakaeri, and other tribes live in or around the park. Some, like the Yora, have only recently been contacted, while others, like the Mascho Piro, have wisely remained in a Stone Age state.

The Yora we met were on their way downriver for some purpose we could not divine; no park guard speaks their particular Panoan dialect. Perhaps it was their recent discovery of fishhooks or of the use of clothes as protection against the biting sandflies that had brought them out of the remote end of the park. The males wore their penises cinched and tied up with cords around their waists. Some were adorned with strings of beads that encircled their faces and were joined to the septums of their noses. Something about their gesticulations made them look unmistakably wild. They are, indeed, a fierce tribe, willing to unleash mighty 7-foot-long (2 m) arrows at other Indians, oil explorers, and lumber prospectors alike. In recent times, they have been gradually encroaching upon the territory of the Machiguenga, one of the other ethnic groups of the area. Only in the past two years have the Yora made peaceful contact with anthropologists and the missionaries who haunt all tropical wilderness areas, hoping to gather souls no matter what the cultural cost.

Such religious zeal has also had an ecological downside. Before the park was created, the missionaries funded their proselytizing by running a poaching and animal-hide export business using Indian labor. The Indian culture, along with the wildlife, was being systematically destroyed until the park service expelled the missionaries and decreed a hands-off policy with regard to the indigenous peoples of Manú. The Indians are now free to live in a traditional manner in the distant reaches of the park. Biologists and all other visitors are forbidden to contact indigenous peoples in order that neither their health nor their cultural equilibrium is imperiled. Nevertheless, we could not avoid the encounter with the Yora, and we took away from it a deeper appreciation of the park and the sanctuary it offers the wildest and most endangered organism: aboriginal humanity. We felt the strangeness of meeting fellow humans who still hunt and fight with bows and arrows, have no conception of what a park is, and do not know what Peru means.

The first night on the river, we camped on a sandbar and had tuna and crackers for supper, items that became dietary staples. A *friaje* wind from the south blew damp, cold air, and the warmer river steamed. As we battled the unexpectedly low temperatures with a bottle of ouzo, Terborgh recounted a story about one of his research trips to New Guinea. After traveling with a group of porters far into the highlands, Terborgh and evolutionary biologist Jared Diamond trudged into camp near a remote village. Terborgh sat down and pulled off his boots. To his amazement, the

The Spix's guan, here resting at its midday roost in Manú National Park, is a favorite game bird because of its large size, high-quality meat, and the relative ease with which it can be shot. With a low reproductive rate, guans disappear rapidly under hunting pressure, and many populations have been extinguished.

simple act sent a swarm of onlooking villagers running into the forest shrieking with fright. One of the more worldly porters explained to the mystified Terborgh: "Them bush kanakas thought you pulling off your feet." The vulnerability of such people cannot be overestimated, and the park plays an important role in thwarting the rapacious tendrils of civilization that first reach into the frontier—gold miners, loggers, coca traffickers, missionaries, and miscellaneous hucksters—and often sponge up profits at the expense of the ancestral inhabitants of the forest.

Ironically, part of the value of the park comes from one of the past incursions into the Manú region. Local accounts and limited historical observations suggest that during the rubber boom that began a century ago, the Manú Indians were ravaged by the ruthless Peruvian rubber baron Carlos Fitzcarraldo. In his battle for rubber territory and in opening a route to the Río Alto Madre de Dios, Fitzcarraldo decimated the Mascho Indian tribes that once lived along the Manú River. Piro Indians were employed to enslave other Indians as labor for rubber tapping. Those who resisted were killed; many others succumbed to epidemics of infectious disease. The rubber boom was short lived, and the traffic of tappers and the strife they caused ceased at the turn of the century. But the Indian population, impoverished as it is and lacking the most basic health care, has not rebounded, and today, there are regions of the park that are emptier than they have been for thousands of years. The depopulated portion of the park is now as close as one can get to the Amazon as it was before any human settlement occurred. Biologists base their work in the depopulated area because the animal communities live in a state as free from human intervention as one can find anywhere.

After two days on the Manú, we pulled up at a beach and began carrying the gear several hundred yards into Cocha Cashu, the field site. The Cocha is a cashew-shaped lake, an old oxbow left by one of the shifts in the meandering river. It resembles a giant, curving trough of pea soup. Our encampment was on floodplain soil, relatively rich alluvial silt that supports the classic, yet rarely encountered, high rainforest. The biggest trees were truly huge, with buttresses as wide as ten yards from side to side. Lianas as thick as the largest ship cables crawled upward to a canopy sixty to seventy yards high. The trees were festooned with strange flowers, some like pink powder puffs erupting from the trunks.

I pitched my tent at the lake edge and awaited my first night in this forest. Promptly at six o'clock, darkness seeped in like tea, filtering around the trees. Huge click beetles with luminous eyespots shining the cool, fluorescent green light of fireflies streaked through the dusk. Night came not as dark emptiness but as a rising cloud of living sound. Thousands of nameless voices broke out, and katydids and crickets began to file their legs and wing combs. They had the percussive, metallic sounds of tambourines, the rhythm of ratchets and castanets. They entered into choruses

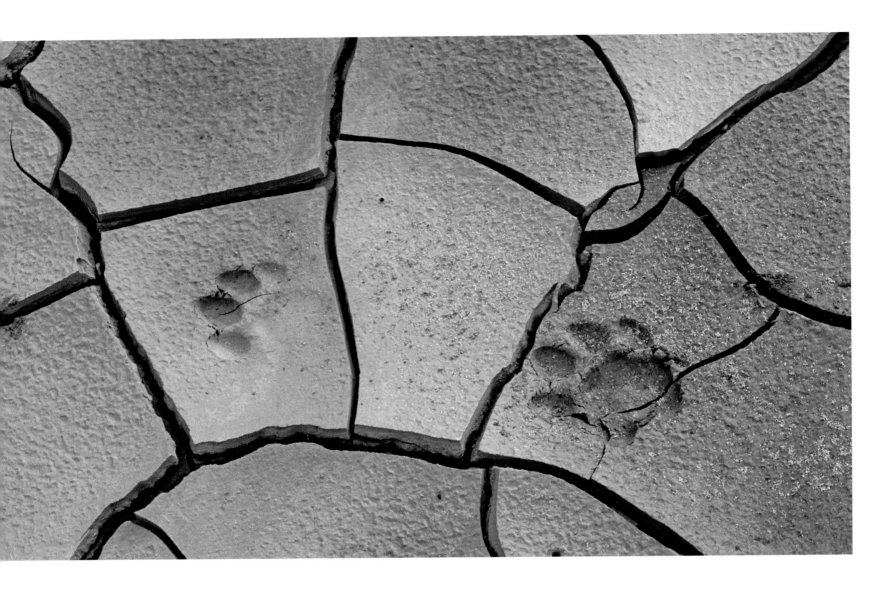

An adult jaguar leaves an unmistakably large paw print, with deep, rounded toe and palm impressions, above.

The gray-winged trumpeter, right, and its relatives forage on the forest floor for fruit knocked to the ground by monkeys, guans, toucans, and other fruit-eating birds. Trumpeters remain common in undisturbed areas of the Amazonian rainforest but are very vulnerable to deforestation and hunting.

of trills and reverberations that had the quality of the radio signals that come echoing in from deep space as you dial the shortwave radio searching for the news of the world. Over the lake, noisy with flopping fish, where the sky was revealed, the Southern Cross lay on its side beside the Milky Way, that luminous flow of stars the native Amazonians call "the River."

As the crescent moon emerged, a strange call resounded nearby, a loud, vomiting *boorkk* that could only be the giant po-too, a night-active bird that bears a remarkable resemblance to the weathered gray ends of the dead snags on which it perches. With its superb camouflage, it was impossible to pick out even with a flashlight. The retching voice issuing invisibly from a spot right above was ominous. Perhaps that is why Peruvians believe the call is a bad omen and have named the bird *ayamama*, a Quechua word meaning "mother of the cadaver." But the bird ceased calling, and I drifted off to sleep under a rain of chittering cries and bits of debris that accompanied a family of night monkeys foraging by the light of the stars and the moon.

In the morning, I awoke with a jolt of adrenaline stimulated by the creaking, tearing sound of a massive tree limb breaking overhead. I scrambled out but saw no sign of impending doom. At breakfast, Cocha Cashu veterans informed me that the sound was nothing more than the display of a piping guan that uses its wing feathers to create the distinctive call. It was a sound I would hear with unusual regularity. Around Cocha Cashu, guans proved to be more abundant than I have seen anywhere else in the New World tropics. Big, meaty birds that usually have a small clutch, they are among the first elements of the avifauna to vanish under hunting pressure. Whenever I flush a guan, I am always amazed by the apparent naïveté of the bird. After its brief, noisy alarm reaction when it flaps and hops up from the ground, its strongest impulse seems to be to get a good look at you from a convenient perch. It makes a target that is hard to miss. But here, it was common to see guans in the forest. I often hiked behind a flock of waddling trumpeters, goose-sized fruit-eating birds that bobbed their white rumps nonchalantly as they foraged just a pace or two ahead, and everywhere plump tinamous scurried along the trails. It was a novel pleasure to have all these big game birds almost underfoot and to hear their songs sung and whistled in strong choruses.

Other animals I had always thought were naturally rare turned out to be present in great numbers. At Cocha Cashu, black spider monkeys, a favored food throughout the Amazon, were not just common, they were brazen, rattling the branches and chucking debris down on me whenever I disturbed them as they fed in a fig tree. The creek beds were churned and muddied by tapirs on their foraging rounds. On the beach, I saw the tracks of the capybara, the largest rodent in the world (150 pounds, or 68 kg), closely followed by a set of jaguar tracks.

Giant otters are another hallmark of Manú's fauna. Prized for their skin, they have been hunted to the brink of extinction. These 7-foot-long (2 m), 70-pound (32 kg) members of the weasel family need space in which to roam and fish. They travel widely from lake to lake along rivers, in groups of four to six adults.

The colorful clown tree frog (*Hyla triangulum*) is one of well over a hundred frog species that occur in Manú National Park.

Martha Brecht Munn, an ecologist who studied giant otters at Manú, found that each animal eats more than one large fish every hour and that the giant otters will kill anacondas 10 feet (3 m) long, attack adult black caimans, and even charge a jaguar if it prowls too close. In concert, they are among the planet's most formidable and ecologically demanding predators. So great are the dietary and spatial requirements of the giant otter that Manú probably supports only one hundred adults. It takes but a single hide hunter to eliminate a population.

The importance of hunting impressed me most deeply when a Machiguenga, a person born and bred in the Peruvian forest, stopped on his way downriver to catch some fish at the Cocha. He hunted with a bow and arrow from a precarious position in a dugout canoe, a thin, tippy proposition under the best of conditions. But he stood erect at the end of the canoe, one foot ahead of the other, a balancing act supreme. He poled himself ahead easily, smoothly, using his 7-foot-long (2 m) bow of black chonta palm (*Bactris* sp.). Through my binoculars from the far shore, I could see him staring at the opaque green surface of the lake. Then he nocked an arrow and let it fly. The arrow bobbed up with a thrashing silver *boca chica* fish impaled on it.

After witnessing that display of skill, I left to do my fieldwork in the forest interior. But Peruvian ornithologist Walter Wurst stayed on to watch the Machiguenga, who shot twenty times and came up with twenty *boca chica*. Later, Wurst and I learned firsthand just what a mysterious art we had witnessed. Naively,

we rounded up a bow and some arrows and set out on a similar mission. I paddled, and Wurst knelt in the bow of the boat ready to harvest our supper. We were utterly defeated by the wily *boca chica*. It was not just that Wurst was not as fine a marksman or that my paddle strokes were less smooth than the Machiguenga's. Our difficulties were far more fundamental: the *boca chica* were completely invisible to us. Long before we could read some sign of their presence, perhaps a bubble rising to the surface, they swirled away. The Machiguenga, having grown up with a bow in his hand and spurred on by absolute necessity, had developed a high level of skill that was not only impressive to us but also completely beyond our perceptual abilities.

Tales of Amazonian Indian hunting skills and woodcraft are legion, but this was the first time I had seen such skill so directly translated into hunting success. With a rifle and a few friends, that same man could decimate wildlife populations with ease if encouraged by the market economy for illegal hides and wild game. Studies in Peru show that a family of settlers, although lacking the great skills of the indigenous people, consumes nearly 2,000 pounds (about 900 kg) of monkeys, macaws, and other game annually. Little wonder, then, that rainforest game soon grows scarce in the presence of humans. I began to realize the importance for the surviving tribes of Manú of the depopulated areas, which act as a generating space that replenishes the depleted game populations around the villages. Instead of the territorial no-man's-land that warfare imposes, the unpopulated area of the park ensures that game populations will continue to be present as long as a large core remains unhunted.

And in Manú, I began to appreciate why animals that seem common elsewhere—small rodents, sloths, opossums—appeared to be scarcer. Terborgh suggests that in Manú, where there are still all the cats, bush dogs, and harpy eagles to keep a close check on them, populations have a more natural balance of numbers than in most other areas now being studied. Here, limber-limbed spider monkeys leapt wildly through the treetops, and the streams were heavily marked with tapir tracks. I heard, for the first time, the *cough-cough* call of the jaguar at night. Macaws, the glorious parrots I had thought to be rare, settled in abundance in the treetops at dawn to gather the first warm rays of light with their brilliant plumage. The lake was jammed with fish, turtles, and caimans.

The significance of such sights was not merely in their beauty. They were a lesson explaining just how limited is our understanding of ecological communities in the tropics. After nineteen years of visiting the tropics, I thought I had a fair idea of the basic composition of tropical ecological communities. But I was more ignorant than I could have imagined.

Such ignorance is common among ecologists, because tropical biology is concentrated in just a few convenient sites in Costa Rica, Panama, and other accessible areas. Almost without exception, the sites are extremely disturbed; their large predator populations and important game species have been radically thinned or eliminated, producing changes we hardly understand. For example, white-lipped peccaries, a social species of pig that requires great expanses of forest habitat, are absent from much of their former range. White-lips are not only major predators but also dispersers of palm seeds, consumers of snakes, and tillers of the soil, and their absence must set off a chain reaction about which we know nothing. As a consequence, what little we do know about tropical ecology is often a biased misimpression. The really significant places go unstudied and are frequently lost to logging and hunting before they are ever known. Terborgh wants to change this. He and his colleagues and students are busy studying the monkeys, macaws, cats, otters, and caimans that have vanished from other parts of Amazonia. But Terborgh also has a dream and a plan that embraces more than just Manú. It is to find the funds required to study ten virgin tropical-forest sites around the world. He sees it as a last-ditch effort to collect the baseline data needed to understand what natural tropical-forest ecosystems are really like before they are irretrievably changed.

One senses his desperation when he writes, "I feel as an astronomer might on being told that the stars were going to burn out in ten years and that there would only be that long to unravel the mysteries of the heavens."

The stars will wait for as long as we may need to grasp their greatness. But Manú, for all its vastness, has a uniqueness that cannot be taken for granted. If we lose this place and the few others like it, all we will retain are the first few preliminary measurements of our ignorance. We will have lost those special places, the true wilderness where biological mystery breathes and grows inviolate, where the firmament of living species still stands unbroken.

Blue-and-yellow macaws live in flocks that require hundreds of square miles of forest. This pair is nesting in the rotting stump of a *Mauritia* palm.

Further reading

Writings on the natural history of the tropical rainforest are vast and fragmented. Where to begin? The early works of natural history remain among the most informative because of their scope. Above all, they express the sense of discovery that all naturalists experience when making their first contact with tropical rainforests. I recommend the following books that focus on the neotropics:

Bates, H.W. *The Naturalist on the River Amazons*. London: John Murray, 1864; reprinted Berkeley: University of California Press, 1962.

Belt, T. *The Naturalist in Nicaragua*. London: 1874; reprinted Chicago: University of Chicago Press, 1985, with a foreword by Daniel H. Janzen.

Spruce, R. *Notes of a Botanist on the Amazon and Andes*, 2 vols., edited by A.R. Wallace. London: Macmillan, 1908; reprinted New York: Johnson Reprints, 1970.

Von Humboldt, A. *Personal Narrative of Travels to the Equinoctial Regions of America*, 3 vols. London: G. Rutledge, 1851.

Wallace, A.R. *A Narrative of Travels on the Amazon and Rio Negro*. London: Ward, Lock and Co., 1889; reprinted New York: Dover, 1972.

Wallace, A.R. *Natural Selection and Tropical Nature*. London: Macmillan, 1895.

Waterton, C. *Wanderings in South America*. London: Century Publishing, 1825; reprinted London: Century Publishing, 1983.

In the twentieth century, a few biologists have continued the narrative tradition. Books I recommend include:

Beebe, W. *Edge of the Jungle*. New York: Henry Holt, 1921.

Carr, A.F. *High Jungles and Low*. Gainesville: University of Florida Press, 1953.

Skutch, A.F. *A Naturalist in Costa Rica*. Gainesville: University of Florida Press, 1971.

Skutch, A.F. *A Naturalist on a Tropical Farm*. Berkeley: University of California Press, 1980.

Most research on tropical ecology is now published on a piecemeal basis in technical scientific journals such as *Biotropica* or *Journal of Tropical Ecology* and in equally specialized books. The academic system does not reward scientists for producing popular accounts of their research, so books that communicate the experience of rainforests are not being produced by the people who know the most about this environment. There are, however, some exceptions, and a few tropical ecologists have published more accessible and personal accounts of their fieldwork. I recommend the following:

Tree frog (*Hyla punctata*), in Manú National Park, Peru.

Goulding, M. *Amazon, The Flooded Forests*. London: BBC Books, 1989.

Snow, D. *The Web of Adaptation*. New York: Demeter Press-Quadrangle, 1976.

Tropical ecologist John Terborgh's book, *Where Have All the Birds Gone?* (Princeton, New Jersey: Princeton University Press, 1989), is another exception to my above generalization.

A uniquely elegant and profound book that discusses tropical fieldwork, the importance of biological diversity, the nature of science, and our relationship to nature is E.O. Wilson's *Biophilia* (Cambridge, Massachusetts: Harvard University Press, 1984).

Those concerned with tropical conservation will find a good introduction in the following books:

Bunker, S.G. *Underdeveloping the Amazon*. Chicago: University of Chicago Press, 1985.

Caufield, C. *In the Rainforest*. London: Heinmann, 1985.

Myers, N. *The Primary Source: Tropical Forest and Our Future*. New York: Norton, 1984.

Soule, M. *Conservation Biology: The Science of Scarcity and Diversity*. Sunderland, Massachusetts: Sinauer, 1986.

Wilson, E. (ed.). *Biodiversity*. Washington, D.C.: National Academy Press, 1988.

For those who wish to delve into tropical ecological research, the following books will get you started, and they contain references to most of the previous important technical literature:

Janzen, D. (ed.). *Costa Rican Natural History*. Chicago: University of Chicago Press, 1983.

Prance, G.T., T. Lovejoy (eds.). *Amazonia*. New York: Pergamon Press, 1985.

In recent years, publishers have produced a number of excellent photography books about rainforests. The following titles, to mention just a few, are very well written, and contain stunning photographs:

Fogden, M., P. Fogden. *Costa Rica: Wildlife of the National Parks and Reserves of Costa Rica*. Costa Rica: Editorial Heliconia, 2005.

Leigh, E., C. Ziegler. *A Magic Web*. New York: Oxford University Press, 2002.

Marent, T., B. Morgan. *Rainforest*. New York: DK Publishing, 2006.

Wolfe, A., G. Prance. *Rainforests of the World: Water, Fire, Earth and Air*. New York: Crown Publishing, 1998.

Acknowledgments

Adrian Forsyth

I would like to thank the following people, agencies, and organizations for providing assistance and information: David Bell, Jim Crisp, Chris Darling, Cynthia Echevarria, Michael and Patricia Fogden, Turid Forsyth, Wolf Guindon, William Haber, Bruce Lyon, John Terborgh, Conservation International, the Monteverde Conservation League, the Peruvian National Park System, the Tropical Science Center, and the World Wildlife Fund Canada.

Michael and Patricia Fogden

Many of the photographs in this book were taken while we were working on various natural history projects and we owe a huge debt to biologist friends who generously shared with us their expertise and enthusiasm for their subjects. We are especially grateful to Martha Crump (frogs), Philip DeVries (butterflies), Peter Feinsinger (hummingbirds), Larry Gilbert (passion flowers and *Heliconius* butterflies), Harry Greene (snakes), Bill Haber (butterflies and plants), Daniel Janzen (moths and caterpillars), Jack Longino (ants), Jay Savage (frogs), Gary Stiles (hummingbirds), and Willow Zuchowski (plants).

We cannot mention everyone else who has ever provided us with information, identifications, logistical support, and congenial company in the field, but the following have been very helpful with the material in this book: Anne Brooke, the late John and Doris Campbell, David and Deborah Clark, Eladio Cruz, Adrian Forsyth, Gordon and Juta Frankie, Luis Diego Gómez, Wilford Guindon, Craig Guyer, Barry Hammel, Peter Jenson of Explornapo and Explorama Lodges in Peru, Liz Jones and Abraham Gallo of Rio Tigre Lodge, Michael Kaye of Costa Rica Expeditions, Richard Laval, Bonifacio de Leon, Bruce Lyon, Bob Matlock, Mario Mendez, Gene Montgomery, Greg and Kathy Murray, Norman Obando, Alan Pounds, George Powell, Alejandro Solorzano, the Tretti family of Rancho La Ensenada, Roberto Wesson, and Jim Wolfe.

We are also indebted to Stephen Johnson for his expert help with our digital images and to Susan Fogden for keeping things running smoothly while we are in the field. Finally, we must thank John McCuen, Marc Roegiers, and Mathias Black of Zona Tropical for their enthusiastic support.